Tom Page

Emotive Design Methods in Product Branding

Tom Page

Emotive Design Methods in Product Branding

Brand and Emotion and their Relationship with Product Design

LAP LAMBERT Academic Publishing

Impressum/Imprint (nur für Deutschland/ only for Germany)

Bibliografische Information der Deutschen Nationalbibliothek: Die Deutsche Nationalbibliothek verzeichnet diese Publikation in der Deutschen Nationalbibliografie; detaillierte bibliografische Daten sind im Internet über http://dnb.d-nb.de abrufbar.

Alle in diesem Buch genannten Marken und Produktnamen unterliegen warenzeichen-, marken- oder patentrechtlichem Schutz bzw. sind Warenzeichen oder eingetragene Warenzeichen der jeweiligen Inhaber. Die Wiedergabe von Marken, Produktnamen, Gebrauchsnamen, Handelsnamen, Warenbezeichnungen u.s.w. in diesem Werk berechtigt auch ohne besondere Kennzeichnung nicht zu der Annahme, dass solche Namen im Sinne der Warenzeichen- und Markenschutzgesetzgebung als frei zu betrachten wären und daher von jedermann benutzt werden dürften.

Coverbild: www.ingimage.com

Verlag: LAP LAMBERT Academic Publishing GmbH & Co. KG
Dudweiler Landstr. 99, 66123 Saarbrücken, Deutschland
Telefon +49 681 3720-310, Telefax +49 681 3720-3109
Email: info@lap-publishing.com

Herstellung in Deutschland:
Schaltungsdienst Lange o.H.G., Berlin
Books on Demand GmbH, Norderstedt
Reha GmbH, Saarbrücken
Amazon Distribution GmbH, Leipzig
ISBN: 978-3-8443-1067-2

Imprint (only for USA, GB)

Bibliographic information published by the Deutsche Nationalbibliothek: The Deutsche Nationalbibliothek lists this publication in the Deutsche Nationalbibliografie; detailed bibliographic data are available in the Internet at http://dnb.d-nb.de.

Any brand names and product names mentioned in this book are subject to trademark, brand or patent protection and are trademarks or registered trademarks of their respective holders. The use of brand names, product names, common names, trade names, product descriptions etc. even without a particular marking in this works is in no way to be construed to mean that such names may be regarded as unrestricted in respect of trademark and brand protection legislation and could thus be used by anyone.

Cover image: www.ingimage.com

Publisher: LAP LAMBERT Academic Publishing GmbH & Co. KG
Dudweiler Landstr. 99, 66123 Saarbrücken, Germany
Phone +49 681 3720-310, Fax +49 681 3720-3109
Email: info@lap-publishing.com

Printed in the U.S.A.
Printed in the U.K. by (see last page)
ISBN: 978-3-8443-1067-2

Emotive Design Methods in Product Branding

Tom Page

Abstract

The aim of this research was to establish how brands can create an emotional relationship with users through the design of their products. Investigations into existing knowledge on brand, emotional design, and branding techniques employed by designers were conducted in the literature review. Further empirical investigations were undertaken to build on the findings presented in the literature.

The literature review highlighted that products can play a significant role in communicating a brand. It was commented that designers can employ product semantics theory to articulate the values of the brand in three dimensions. The literature review also found users become attached to products which share the same values as them and communicate a desired image. Furthermore, emotional attachment occurs if the product is related to memories and past associations. These findings however were with respect to objects in general, with further research required to investigate how branding could affect these findings. Current methods used by working product designers were also sought to compare against those presented in the literature.

Interviews were conducted with users to identify how the ideas presented in the literature would hold when investigating branded products specifically. Mobile phones were highlighted as an object of emotional attachment in the literature and were used as an example in investigating how the users become attached to both the product and the brand. The brand values of mobile phone manufacturers were identified in case studies and were benchmarked against the views presented by the users in the interviews. It was found that users bought or aspired to buy products from brands which share the same values as them. Brands are able to connect emotionally to users in the same way objects do, through association and memory.

Interviews with designers revealed that semiotic analysis is undertaken to develop a brand's visual language. Semiotics is the investigation into cultural meanings of the keywords. These meanings are used to dictate an image search which is used as reference material when designing products. Users are not involved in this process because it may infringe on client confidentiality.

The findings show that brands are able to make an emotional relationship by using the product to communicate its values and aspirations of the user. The branded product has not been shown to be significant in isolation, but acts as a link for the brand to connect to the user to create association and build memories of the experiences shared between the brand and users.

Contents

Acknowledgements

We would like acknowledge and thank Dr. Howard Denton for his continued help and assistance in this research work. We would also like to acknowledge the designers from PDD, Vibrant Form, DCA Design, V2 Studios, and Hyphen Design for their participation in telephone interviews. We would like to thank the six participants who took part in the interviews.

Introduction

1.1 Study Introduction

As western society moves increasingly to a service based economy, consumers have a broader choice than ever in their purchase decisions. The economic base is now moving from production, to consumption. As the New York Times suggests, 'It has gravitated from the sphere of rationality to the realm of desire; from the objective to the subjective; to the realm of psychology.' (New York Times 2009).Watching a film on television is now a 'cinema viewing experience', and ice creams are marketed as 'utter indulgence'. The lower levels of human needs, outlined by Maslow (1986) (see fig 1), are largely fulfilled in the developed world with impulses now based upon the higher hedonic goals of self actualisation.

Figure 1 –Maslow's Hierarchy of Needs,
Anon 2009, Net 1

This shift in consumer behaviour has changed how products are marketed (Gobe 2001). The features of a product or what 'make' it is, are now less important than how it makes the consumer *feel*. The tangible assets of a company are now seen as less valuable than the intangible. An obvious example is Coca- Cola, their market gap including brand value is $120 Billion, and their market gap not including brand value is $50 Billion. The brand and the emotional associations people have with the company are now the key elements which influence a consumer's purchase decisions (Gobe 2001).

This study will investigate the role of products in creating the emotional perceptions of a brand. Product designs which create a lasting emotional bond between brand and user to provoke further purchases may be crucial to keep consumers interested and support the future economy.

1.2 Study Aims

The aim of this research work is to investigate how brands emotionally engage users through the design of their products.

1.3 Study Objectives

In order to achieve the aims of the study, there were five objectives to complete-

- To define what a brand is
- To see how brand strategy and product design relate to each other
- To investigate how objects can evoke emotion
- To identify the methodologies used by designers to communicate a brand's values through products

- To identify how people become attached to branded products

1.4 Key Questions

In order to complete the study objectives it was necessary to define a set of research questions. These questions would be used to guide the investigation of previous work and the empirical research phase. The key questions were:

- What is a brand?
- How does a company's branding strategy relate to the design of their products?
- How do products trigger an emotional response from users?
- What tools are used by designers to articulate the values of a brand through products?
- How do people become attached to branded objects?

1.3 Study Structure

This report is composed of seven chapters, starting with and introduction outlining the aims and objectives of the study. Chapter 2 focuses on the prior work in the literature review and draws conclusions on with respect to the research questions. Chapter 3.0 details the methodology to be followed in conducting the empirical research. Case studies to act as a benchmark to the findings in the user interviews are presented in chapter 4.0. Chapter 5.0 reports on the findings from the semi-structured interviews, exploring how users become attached to branded objects. Chapter 6.0 presents the findings from the semi-structured telephone interviews with designers. The results from the interviews and case study are discussed in comparison to the findings from the literature in chapter 7.0. The studies final conclusions as well as recommendations for further study are commented upon in chapter 8.0

2.0 Literature Review

Introduction-

2.1 What is a brand?

The notion of a 'brand' is currently a point of disagreement between experts with no two definitions meaning the same thing. One idea presented by Neumeier (2008) is that a brand is a person's gut feeling about a product, service, or company. He argues that a brand is neither a logo nor corporate identity, as these are just symbols of a brand. Moreover, it is a platonic ideal, suggesting it is what society and consumers consider it to be, rather than what is inflicted upon them by a company. Keller (2008) also promotes this concept, suggesting a brand is a collection of mental associations related to a product or service held by customers. Brands which successfully communicate their message are those whose projected meaning is the same as the meaning interpreted by consumers.

Zyman (2006) however, interprets the notion of a brand as the building of sensorial experiences over time. This idea has developed as the nature in which brands communicate with users have changed, notably with the introduction of the internet. This has provided new platforms to allow companies to sensually engage with users through sight, sound and touch. Zyman (2006) comments that Apple (see Figure 2) has equally stimulated these senses, in each of its products, over a number of years, allowing it to be distinguishable from its competition.

Figure 2 – Apple Mac, Davies 2009, Net 2

Opinion is gathering in this direction, as Lindstrom (2007) comments that a brand which is successful is one which conveys a widely recognised sensory experience, as a broad way of spreading its values. Intel, for example, has harnessed the sense of sound with its distinct and memorable jingle for over ten years, even though the brand's core offer is not associated with audio in any way. Emotional relationships with users are therefore created by exploiting the senses successfully and engaging the target user. This opinion is also held by Richard Seymour of design consultancy Seymour Powell. He regards branding as a series of promises that do not change over time (Seymour 2008)

The concept of a 'brand' is therefore considered to be highly based on experience and is driven by sensorial responses. Time and consistency are highlighted as important factors. A definition 'brand' may therefore be a consistent emotional response to a company, through the senses, over time.

2.2 Product design as part of brand communication

Kapferer (2008) has established a model to describe the relationship between products and the brands which frame them, based upon three poles (see fig 3):

The product experience

Brand Communication

Brand Name and associations

Brand Concept 'the big idea'

Figure 3- Kapferer's three poles of brand communication

- Brand name and associations
- Brand concept or 'the big idea'
- The product or service experience

Each of these elements is equal in its communication of a brand and its values to customers. For Kapferer (2008), a brand cannot be discussed as singular elements such as a typeface or product, but as a "living system of cumulative brand experience". (Kapferer 2008 pp 25-26). What unifies both product and brand is the common vision and spirit embodied in both aspects, rather than a logo or common visual entity.

This opinion is held by many other commentators and is widely considered to be a common paradigm when discussing products and brands, particularly by those with a marketing background. An example of this is presented by Schmitt (1997), who describes the public face of brands, as four P's; Properties, Products, Presentations and Publications (see fig 4).

brand communication

Properties

Products

Presentations

Publications

Figure 4- Schmitt's four P's of brand
communication

Much like Kapferer has outlined three equal poles, Schmitt argues that each element must be treated equally to communicate a coherent message (Schmitt 1997).

Difficulties in the inclusion of design in a brand strategy are however identified by Schmitt (1997), suggesting creativity cannot be measured and therefore aesthetic evaluation systems cannot be established .Organisations aiming to implement aesthetic strategies are unable to objectively measure the results (Schmitt 1997). Schmitt fails to offer suggestion as to how this can be resolved, and one might argue it results in unnecessarily narrow and biased conclusions from a marketer. Rich (2009) however, mediates between the two viewpoints, suggesting that a way to combat this is for designers to implement an evidence-based methodology to justify design decisions.

The success of a product due to the brand has again been discussed in the work of Kapferer (2008). Historically, most brands are born out of a product or service innovation which outperforms its competitor's . In order to become the 'leading brand', companies need not have the best product with respect to performance (Kapferer 2008). The example of Swatch watches illustrates his point, stating customers 'buy convenience and style, not long lasting superior performance' (Kapferer 2008, p 19).

Figure 5- Swatch Watch, Swatch 2009, Net 18

This is inconsistent with him presenting the product as one of three equal poles in the communication of brand. Highlighting 'convenience and style', Kapferer also implies the emotional factors at play in the appeal of a brand.

A recent comparison between Sony and Panasonic is illustrated by Grinyer (2009) who further stresses the importance of the designed product. Both have a turnover of approximately $62 billion a year. Sony is recognised for innovation, whereas Panasonic prefers to follow industry trends (Grinyer 2009). Sony has had a long established innovations centre and a design led focus within the company (Sony 2009). Consequently, Interbrand (2009) have put Sony's brand ranking at $12 Billion in comparison to Panasonic at around $4 Billion.

2.6 Semantics and 3D branding strategies

For a brand to differentiate from the competition, it is contended by Karjalainen that visual consistency over their product line is crucial (Karjalainen 2007). Similarly, Page and Herr agree that by developing designs which are visually similar, a company can significantly enhance their brand's communication (Page & Herr 2002).

It is widely considered by design theorists that the concept of product semantics is central to the manifestation of a brand's values in a 3d form such as Verzeyer who comments:

"Brands communicate to users through products. Products adopt a place in society. They embody social and cultural meanings. This is the realm of product semantics, communicating meaning through form" (Veryzer 1998, pp99).

2.6.1 Models of semantic application-

The application of semantic theory to design practise essentially follows a single school of thought , which is built around two stages, firstly *analysis*, and secondly *translation*.

Table 1-Models of semantic Application

	Analysis	*Translation*
Karjalainen	-Different visual elements ranked in significance	- Most significant traits applied widely
Warrell	-Identification of explicit design cues -Identification of implicit cues	-Apply explicit cues scarcely - NOT IDENTIFIED

Analysis

Karjalainen (2007) proposes a method which is built around two stages .The first stage is the 'Analysis of brand characteristics and design cues' (Karjalainen 2007, pp 16). There are two types of design cues; explicit cues and implicit cues (see fig 6). Explicit design cues are the obvious visual features intended to be easily recognised in a brand (Karjalainen 2003). In order for brands to become recognisable, they simply repeat them from product to product (Karjalainen 2007). Implicit values are the philosophical, deeper associations people have with brands.

Figure 6- Application of Explicit cues, (Karjalainen 2003)

This draws parallels to the method proposed by Warrell. The first major stage in his methodology requires deconstructing a brand's form into respective visual elements (Warell 2001).

Translation

The second stage in the methodology proposed by Karjalainen is 'Transforming brand Character to Product Design', whereby the explicit and implicit design cues are translated into 3-dimentional forms (Karjalainen 2007 pp 19). Karjalainen adds that explicit cues are scarcely used, as they do not often transfer well across different products and are often context sensitive (Karjalainen 2007). Implicit cues however are used more often, as they are more loosely defined and therefore more easily transferable to numerous product categories (Karjalainen 2007). Karjalainen fails to identify how these implicit, less tangible cues are actually applied to the design of a product. Similarly, Warrell (2001) proposes his second stage, 'Product Form Synthesis', whereby the different visual elements are applied in a hierarchical manner; the most significant being applied widely and the least significant scarcely (Warell 2001, pp23).

Karjalainen suggests the downfall of these methods is their subjective nature, as the selection of features, their weighting, and application is down to the opinion of either a design team or user, and not with exact measurements (Karjalainen 2007). This can be linked with Schmitt's (2001) earlier criticism of the role of design in brand strategy, again for its inability to be measured objectively.

These methods are proposed by design academics from Universities, and not from design professionals. Clearly there is scope for further empirical research which identifies the methods used by successful designers in leading design consultancies. Furthermore, these approaches fail to identify how they would change in different circumstances and do not suggest how flexible they are. For example, the design of a new television for a leading brand may require a different aesthetic approach than one for an emerging brand with limited existing products in its range to refer to. The literature to date also fails to identify how a new brand language is developed initially, rather than just applying existing visual traits to a new product.

Athanakar's (2001) method goes one stage further by involving relevant users to both select and apply the visual cues .By including users at each stage, a more accurate prediction of its affect on the market can be ascertained. (Athankar 2001). However, Athankar's research is now 8 years old, and is again from academia. This reinforces the need to conduct further research to discover what real techniques are used by designers.

2.4 The articulation of emotional design

Recently, psychologists and writers have theorised on the relationship between users and products. Maslow (1989) identifies a three stage process to describe how people respond to products based on physical, intellectual and spiritual needs . Norman (2004) similarly suggests there are three levels of cognitive processing. First, visceral; the immediate judgment of good or bad .Second, behavioural; subconscious thoughts and actions and third, reflective; the conscious and contemplative thoughts (Norman 2004).Panzar (2000) interprets these three levels as play, consumption and life cycle experience. Designer Burnette (1990) describes this phenomenon through seven stages which influence a user's response.

Table 2- Models of emotional interpretation

		Product in use		Emotional Interpretation	
Norman	Visceral	Behavioural		Reflective	
Maslow	Physical	Intellectual		Spiritual	
Panzar	As play	As work		Lifestyle Experience	
Burnette	Emperical Cognate Contextural Functional Evaluative			Emotional Cultural	

These four writers' interpretations can essentially be broken down into two stages-

1) Product in use- User's response based on use and performance
2) Emotional interpretation- The emotional interaction with a product

2.5.1 Emotional Interpretation and self image

The most critical area to this study is the idea of emotional interpretation. Norman describes that design at this level is about fulfilling emotional needs and establishing one's self image world (Norman 2004). The issue of identity sits within the realm of emotional design. As Norman states-'Beauty comes from the reflective level, from the conscious reflection and experience. It is influenced by knowledge, learning and culture' (Norman 2004, pp25). Esslinger, founder of Frog Design, continues this suggestion, offering that customers buy products for self actualising value and experience, not just as functional products (Sweet 1999).

This idea of emotional pleasure linking to emotional needs and self image is also demonstrated by Khaslavsky (1999), who describes the idea of product pleasure as seduction. Successful products are those which provoke the imagination of the user, adopting values which are in tune with those the user has or aspires to. Khaslavsky (1999) describes three steps to emotional engagement; enticement, relationship and fulfilment.

The example used by Khaslavsky (1999) to describe her points is Philippe Starck's juicy salif lemon squeezer.

Figure 7- Juicy Salif Lemon Squeezer,(strangeharvest 2009), net 19

To entice the user, it diverts attention by use of a design not typical to those found in kitchens, creating curiosity (Khaslavsky 1999). Once the user is absorbed, a relationship with the object is built by espousing the values of elegance and sophistication to the user, promising to make a simple action extraordinary (Khaslavsky 1999).

To fulfil final promises and end the experience with the product in a significant way, the lemon squeezer serves as a conversation starter and a point of surprise for those associated to the user, further connoting the *values* the user identifies with (Khaslavsky 1999). It can be noted here the example used, the juicy salif, is not strictly a branded product and is not part of a brand strategy.

2.5.2 Symbolic Meaning to User

Csikszentmihalyi (1981) comments that an object is symbolic in relation to the owner and their environment. The products people display in their homes can suggest meaning and say a lot about who we are (Csikszentmihalyi 1981).

"Household objects constitute an ecology of signs that reflect, as well as shape, the pattern of the owners self" (Csikszentmihalyi 1981 p.26)

An example of this could be a certificate, symbolic of achievement. Norman (2004) highlights a souvenir is another example, symbolic of a holiday or trip, acting as a source of memory or associations.

Csikszentmihalyi (1981) presents the point that objects are symbols of status. From the ancient spear to the modern car, objects are symbols that reflect status to the community and ourselves. Objects can have meaning and, in turn, affect our emotions (Csikszentmihalyi 1981).

Hill (2008) continues the concept of object symbolism, suggesting cars also reflect our self image, in the same way our homes, pets or other possessions signify status, personality, class or outlook on life.

Current studies in the area of emotional design have failed however to state the effect of *branded* products on the emotional states of users. Wallins (2003) highlights that branding is a tool to underline your own self perception, and Norman (2004) has identified products are bought for self actualisation and experience. However, although these statements are linked, there is no single study which considers the effect of a *branded* product on user pleasure. It may be deduced from the literature to date that a branded product will offer emotional value through experience and reflected image, but further research to confirm this will be necessary

2.7 Emotional attachment to objects.

Csikszentmihalyi's (1981) investigations into the relationships of objects and users revealed that furniture was considered by Americans to be the most special object in their homes. Memories and experiences were highlighted as contributing factors for why people were most attached to them. Table 1 shows other objects and their ranking

Table 3-Csikszentmihalyi's (1981), Special objects in American homes

Objects		Percentage
1.	Furniture	36
2.	Visual Art	26
3.	Photographs	23
4.	Books	22
5.	Stereo	22
6.	Musical Instrument	22
7.	TV	21
8.	Sculpture	19
9	Plants	15
10.	Plates	15

The relevance of this data today remains to be investigated. Stereos are listed as the fifth most cherished item, however the current popularity of mp3 players and modern home entertainment systems are likely to change this. Marketing Week magazine have recently ranked mobile phones and cars as the products which offer the greatest opportunity for emotional engagement with users (Marketing Weekly 2009). Csikszentmihalyi (1981) continues to state that objects have meaning to people when they are interpreted through past experiences. This idea is expanded upon by Hekkert (2000) who explains that the extent to which a product evokes memories directly correlates with the level of consumer-product emotional attachment.

It is argued by Chapman (2005) that for an object to become emotionally durable, it should be designed to grow old gracefully with the user. This theory could be applied to the design of any of the objects listed in table 1. He continues to state that products suffer from a condition known as the 'honeymoon period' as a consequence of today's flatpack society.

Chapman (2005) highlights the Tamagotchi craze as an example of widespread emotional attachment to objects. He suggests that the key underpinning of the Tamagotchi was that it could die, which fed a sense of responsibility. This made the bond between product and user stronger, with adults and children becoming seriously engaged with the well being of the virtual pet. Chapman (2005) argues that this primal urge to nurture could elevate user-object interactions in the future if the simulation is perceived as genuine and not transparently gadget-like, creating deeper methods of user engagement. The problem with the Tamagotchi however was it demanded a disproportionate amount of care and attention for the ease with which it died, prompting customers to abandon their pixelated pets (Chapman 2005).

Chapman (2005) also identifies the concept of 'Phantile Drives',. These are the hard to articulate gestures each product suggests. He uses the example of the Apple Power Mac G4 Cube, which glows blue when a hand draws within a few millimetres of it (Chapman 2005). This level of user-product interaction transcends clumsy touch interface and suggests a consciousness and even intelligence from the object which acknowledges our presence (Chapman 2005).

2.8 Literature Review Conclusions

It is clear from the literature that both branding and objects are able to appeal to users emotionally, either by communicating directly to them or by reflecting self image and values. The significance of design in communicating and enhancing a brand's values and image is also highlighted. Consistency, both in terms of visual elements, and brand message, are suggested as crucial for a brand to communicate its message successfully.
However, the writer's have defined this phenomenon in fairly broad terms and have not made a direct example of the link between brand, product, and emotional outcome, but more as disparate elements which can be linked and share similar qualities. Clearly there is scope for further empirical research to investigate this as a single phenomenon.

Emotional attachment to *products* is suggested to occur if the product is linked to memories or past experience; however, there is no research on how *brands* can harness this to their advantage in their products. Further research will aim to establish if memories with a brand's objects have created an emotional relationship.

The appropriateness of the approaches outlined by Karjalainen and Warrell has also been seen to lack suitability in different situations, and further research into the real world techniques employed by practising industrial designers will need to be obtained. The role of the user in the development of a brand language remains to be fully established. As it is ultimately their emotional response towards the product which (in part) creates the relationship with the brand, their role needs to be identified.

3.0 Methodology

3.1 Introduction

The empirical research required falls into two categories. The first was to investigate how users become attached to branded products. The second was to further investigate the tools and methods used by designers to articulate the values of a brand through design.

3.2 Strategy Selection

3.2.1 Eliciting Data from Users

A questionnaire would have been suitable to obtain a wide range of data from a broad range of users. However, this method was rejected as it would not allow for deep interrogation of answers from users, offering only superficial information. (Denscombe 2007)

Running a focus group with several users would also have been applicable to this study. This would have allowed for all the data to be collected efficiently from several users. However, this method was also discarded, as there was the possibility of one person dominating the group and influencing the responses from other informants. (Robson 1999)

It was established that one to one semi structured interviews would be appropriate for this strand of the investigation. This would allow for impromptu questions on interesting points and the opportunity for scrutiny of answers to gain thorough insight. These interviews would be easier to control than a group interview, and would be easier to arrange.

3.2.2 Eliciting Data from Industrial Designers/Design Researchers

In order to investigate further the methods used by industrial designers first hand, there were several research methods that could have been used:

- Postal/web based questionnaire
- Case study
- Semi-structured interview

A questionnaire would have been a feasible method as this could have been issued to many design companies with the prospect of gaining a wide range of information in return. It would also have been an inexpensive and quick method of obtaining empirical data. However, this investigation will require sufficient depth in order to compare and contrast the subtleties of several techniques used by designers. The questionnaire method also lends itself to inaccurate and dishonest responses, and may have been ignored by busy design professionals. (Denscombe 2007)

Conducting a case study would also have been an appropriate method. This would have investigated the processes used in several different design projects, with each project being an example of designing brand languages in different circumstances. (Robson 1999) However, it is unlikely a design consultancy would have allowed any thorough investigation into a project to protect their client's confidentiality.

Semi structured interviews were therefore identified as the most appropriate method of research. Primarily, this was because they would offer the most in depth form of interrogation, and are flexible in nature, allowing the questions to develop as the interview progressed. (Denscombe 2007)

3.3 Phase 2- User Interviews

3.3.1 Interview Aims

The aims of the interview are to identify how participants become attached to branded products, by completing the following objectives-

- To investigate if past experiences and memories with objects are contributing factors to emotional attachment.

- To further the work of Norman and Khaslavsky, and confirm a correlation between the values of the user and the values of the brand.

3.3.2 Interview Structure

The interviews were to be one to one and semi structured, based upon an outlined set of questions in the discussion guide (see appendix A).This was to allow for the respondent to elaborate on their responses, and for the interviewer to interrogate further on interesting points as they arise. The informants were to be questioned on their relationship with their mobile phones, as this was highlighted in the literature, along with cars, as one of the most emotionally engaging products. Mobile phones are also widely owned and easily transportable, facilitating their use in the interviews.

Six participants were recruited, as suggested by Denscombe (2007), of different ages to represent a varied population.

Table 4-Sample population for user interview

	Age	Sex	Status
A	23	Male	Student
B	14	Male	Secondary education
C	54	Female	Full-time employment
D	32	Female	Full-Time employment
E	40	Female	Self Employed
F	63	Male	Retired

The discussion guide would act as a prompt to frame the discussion and to assist in retaining focus. The interviews were to be held in person and were limited to forty minutes in length, to allow for lengthy discussion, but short enough to ensure the remained focus. Participants were made aware the conversation would be recorded with a Dictaphone for transcription.
The participants would also be asked to state the brand of their mobile phone prior to the interview to assist with the case studies.

In preparation for the interview, the participants would be asked to complete a 'brand board', which would facilitate them in expressing the significance of the brand of their phone. Imagery which was felt to be associated with the brand would be collated and stuck on the board. The layout of this board can be found in appendix B.

3.3.3 Interview Analysis

The interviews were to be transcribed. Transcriptions of the interviews can be found in Appendix D. Themes and relationships were to be identified. All data collected was kept anonymous and stored in accordance with Data Protection guidelines.

3.4 Phase 1 -Case Studies-Brand

3.4.1 Case study aims and objectives

Case studies were conducted on the brands of the user's mobile phones to identify the values they wish to communicate. These will be ascertained by identifying brand values taken directly from the brand's literature, such as websites and publications.

3.4.2 Case study analysis

The case studies were analysed in order to make comparisons with:

- How the users interpret the brand in the interview

- To help compare the users values with those of the brand of their mobile phone

3.5 Phase 3- Semi structured interviews with Professional Industrial Designers/Design Researchers

The empirical research will aim to identify if the methodologies proposed by Karjalainen and Warrell are relevant in different situations in professional design practise. Current information from practising industrial designers/design researchers was therefore required.

3.5.1 Interview Aims and objectives

The aims of the interviews were to:

- Gain insight into the methods used by designers to formulate and execute a visual brand language of a product, in several different situations.

- The importance of involving target users in the development of brand languages also needed to be established.

3.5.2 Interview Structure

The interviews were to be semi structured to allow for the designer/design researcher to elaborate and articulate their responses freely, whilst maintaining a focus on the intended topic areas. The interviews were conducted with five participants from leading design consultancies.

Table 5-Sample population for interviews with designers

Participant	Design Company
A	PDD
B	Vibrandt Form
C	DCA Design
D	V2 Studios
E	Hyphen Design

It should be noted here the researcher had pre-established contact with these designers prior to the study. This greatly facilitated the search for participants.

The interviews were to be held on the telephone, as extra travel to several design companies would have incurred significant costs in both time and money. The interviews were restricted to 15 minutes in length to ensure the informant remained focused and not become irritable. It was made explicit the conversation would be recorded by Dictaphone. The informant was also made aware the all information would remain anonymous.

To identify how the designers' methodologies would differ in different scenarios, three hypothetical situations presented to the designers:

1- A well established brand wishes to design a new product to fit in with their existing design language. (For example, a new Sony television to fit in with an existing range of televisions.

2- A well establish brand wishes to create a new design language and apply it to a range of new products .(e.g. Sony wants a new brand language for its range of televisions)

3- A less known/new brand with no specified brand language wishes to formulate and apply a new brand language to a range of products, both now and in the future.

A further question will be asked to investigate the importance of users in the development of brand languages was required.

3.5.3 Interview Analysis

Each interview with designers was to be transcribed. Transcriptions of the interviews can be found in Appendix E. Themes within their answers, and contradictions in their approaches to branding products were to be looked for. The role of the user in their methodologies was also to be identified.

3.5.4 Sample Interview

The discussion guide for the interview can be found in appendix C.

4.0 Case Study Exploration

4.1 Introduction

The purpose of the case studies was to identify the values the mobile phone brands wish to communicate. These will act as a benchmark against the findings from the user interviews. The six informants from the interviews identified Nokia, Motorola, Sony Ericsson and Apple as the brands of their chosen brands. The information for these case studies was taken directly from brand literature.

4.2 Nokia

The values which Nokia promote to communicate their business and philosophy are-

Figure 8- Nokia Brand Values, Nokia
2009, Net 6

'Engaging You' - Nokia aims to satisfy all its customers completely and engage them completely in what Nokia stands for (Nokia 2009)

'Achieving Together' -Nokia outlines trust and connectivity as crucial to progress together (Nokia 2009)

'Very Human' -Environmental responsibility and a sensitive approach to technology are promoted by the company (Nokia 2009)

'Passion for Innovation' -Nokia wishes to be seen as innovating through technology and deeply understanding its users (Nokia 2009)

4.3 Motorola

Figure 9- Motorola Brand Values

Excellence- Motorola wishes to be regarded as the market leader in technology and performance (Motorola 2009)

A Dynamic Future-The 'spirit of invention' is a value Motorola wish to be synonymous with its brand (Motorola 2009)

Responsibility-Environmental responsibility and careful consideration for those who interact with the brand are championed by Motorola. (Motorola 2009)

4.4 SonyEricsson

Figure 10-SonyEricsson Brand values

'Creating Sparks' - Sony Ericsson aims to entertain people as they are mobile to create a rewarding user experience (SonyEricsson 2009)

'Building Connections' - SonyEricsson identifies connecting to new people and starting new relationships as an important value (SonyEricsson 2009)

'What if...?' -SonyEricsson prides itself on being seen to be asking questions and being curious.
'
'Inspiring Beauty' - Sony Ericsson wishes to express the importance beautiful design and 'emotional fulfilment' (SonyEricsson 2009) as a cornerstone of its brand philosophy.

4.5 Apple

Simplicity (Apple 2009) Apple highlights simplicity as one of its core competencies, both in the visual execution of its brand and in the use of its products (Apple 2009).

Fun and Humour (Apple 2009)

Apple aims to make every touch point with its brand as delightful and inspiring as possible. (Apple 2009)

Memorable and Different (Apple 2009)

Apple wishes to delight those who come into contact with the brand by leaving a lasting and thoughtful message with its users. (Apple 2009)

4.0 Phase 2- Interviews with users

4.1 Introduction

The following sections provide a summation of the key insights that have been made. Some are consistent across a number of the participants, where as others are often unique to an individual. Transcriptions of the interviews can be found in appendix D.

4.2 Memories and past experiences with brands.

The brands which users returned to were those which were able to deliver the same benefits as the first time. Participant E describes their past experience with Nokia:

'I'm just so used to the menus and layout of it. The menus on the one I've got now are pretty much the same as the ones which were on the first phone I had 8 years ago'

Four out of the six participants displayed fondness towards Nokia because it was able to deliver the same interaction experience as it had done years before through previous handsets. A further reason why it was seen as a respected brand was due to reliability, as participant A commented:

'I've always stuck with that (Nokia) because it's reliable. They even look reliable. I know what to expect with them'

4.3 Attachment to phone

All participants highlighted that they would not be upset if they lost their mobile phone, providing the sim-card and their numbers were safe. The physical product was not classed as significant. Interstingly, five of the participants expressed that they would feel upset or ashamed if the phone was damaged. All five said they would not replace a damaged phone, suggesting it had now acquired individuality, with the scratches differentiating it from other phones of its kind.

Participants A and E positively argued that by having damage to their phone, it had obtained a level of emotional significance:

'I don't mind having it (the dent) on my phone. It's like a scar. They're interesting.'

'It's got a huge crack on it actually on the back, which I feel a bit upset about, but I don't want another one as it wouldn't feel like my phone'

The *event* of damaging can therefore be seen as a memory the users had with the phone, giving the phone an emotional significance over pristine, well kept phones.

4.4 Values and image

There was a clear correlation between the values of the brand and the values four of the participants sought. Three participants who owned Nokia handsets highlighted reliability was of great importance to them. Similarly, a pillar of Nokia's brand values is 'Achieving Together' (Nokia 2009), which aims to create trust and confidence between itself and users. Participant D commented usability was important, which corresponded with the values presented by Apple.

Respondent B did not choose their current SonyEricsson phone as it was given to them by a relative for free. The participant had negative associations with the SonyEricsson brand, commenting it was a 'geek brand with too many functions' (Respondent B). The participant highlighted simplicity and ease of use as values they sought from phone brands. This correlated with their choice of Apple as their next intended phone purchase.

4.5 Consistency

Brands which were perceived for having a consistent image across their product range were held in high regard. Samsung was shown by three participants to have positive associations, not because of their mobile phones, but because their televisions and audio equipment were able to communicate a desirable message. Participant B commented:

'The rest of their range is cool, I don't need to know all the individual phones look like in my head, because the all Samsung stuff is gorgeous, like their tellys, I know that their phones will look quite cool as well'

It was assumed by the participants the mobile phones would offer the same, regardless if the participant was unable to recall either seeing or using a Samsung phone. Conversely, brands which were considered to communicate less effectively across their range of products were considered with lower esteem. Participants B and D highlighted the (Motorola) 'Pebble' as a desirable phone, yet neither participant was actually able to identify the phone as a Motorola. Participant D suggested Motorola was a 'utility' brand, and could not see the connection with the Pebble phone. Participant B was unable to offer any associations with the Motorola brand, neither spoken nor illustrated with the brand board:

'I can't say I associate anything with them. I couldn't tell you what another one of their phones looks like'

5.0 Phase 2- Telephone Interview with product designers/design researchers

5.1 Introduction

The following sections provide a summary of the key findings from the telephone interviews. Transcriptions of the interviews can be found in appendix D.

5.2 Designing brand languages in different circumstances

Question 1- *"A well established brand wishes for you to aesthetically redesign n x product for them to fit in with their existing range. Can you briefly outline the methodology used to apply their brand traits on this product?"*

At this stage, the respondents highlighted the client would deliver a document to the design team, 'brand guidelines' of the range for the new design is to comply with. Brand guidelines are used to ensure the company's visual branding is used consistently. This includes colour palettes, typography, and surface finishes. Three of the respondents were from larger design consultancies (sixty+ staff) and two of the respondents were from small consultancies (less than ten). The nature of their organisation effected how they approach this task. The larger consultancies would begin by examining how effective the existing brand guidelines are, highlighting areas of weakness or fault. This was intended to result in the inclusion of their redesign into the brief, and generating more income. Design development would then be expected to continue as usual, taking into account the existing, or modified language from the client.

Question2- *"A well established brand wishes to progress/develop their existing brand language and apply it to a new product or range of products. Can you briefly outline the methodology used?"*

The respondents commented this scenario would usually occur if the brand wishes to move to a new market area, such as luxury, or usability. The brand guidelines would again be used but much more loosely. Other factors such as date of release, time on the market, and understanding which products are due to be developed were highlighted as crucial. Respondent B commented further, saying:

'scale and nature of the product is important, as the same language cannot be applied literally to a sponge as it could to a vacuum cleaner for example.'

The methodology followed by larger consultancies would generally be:

1-Identififcation of keywords
-The client's marketing teams would identify keywords to illustrate what the brand wanted to say with this product, such as 'elegant' or 'approachable' in tune with its overall brand communication. The naming of the product range is sometimes introduced here to influence the language, with respondent A using the example of the Motorola 'Razor' to illustrate this.

2-Identify cultural meaning of keywords (semiotics)
-The respondents from the large consultancies were unanimous in identifying the use of **semiotics** in their methodologies. Respondent C describes this as:

'Finding out what the keywords mean culturally, what the cultural baggage of the language is. It's about finding the layers of meaning from these keywords'.

The respondents commented these meanings vary across cultural, consumer segment and product categories. The design team would present several interpretations of a word to the client, each with different images of forms, products and text to illustrate the differences in meaning. Respondent A continued to explain this using the example of the Motorola 'Razor', saying:

'Razor could be cold. It could be deadly. Or it could mean precision. What we have to do is discover which is the most relevant for that market segment at that time'.

3-Concept generation

All three of the designers from the large consultancies highlighted that the first concepts generated would initially be examples of the new design language and not of 'resolved products'. These designs were essentially just capturing the meaning from the semiotics in product form. There were usually several different interpretations of a design language presented, for example 'razor means precise' or 'razor means dangerous', each with 3-5 example products shown.

Smaller consultancies would follow the first stage using keywords but would look for relevant imagery to refer to when designing. They would not undertake any semiotics work to discover meaning. Up to 7 example products would be presented in sketch format to give the client lots of options to choose from. Respondent D commented:

'It is more efficient for us to present loads of concepts around a loose theme, and then for the client to decide which bits of each they like. We don't do anything academic like semantics or anything'.

Question3- *"A new company with no particular brand language wishes for you to aesthetically (re)design x product for them. Can you outline the methodology used to establish their values in 3 dimensions? "*

The methodologies outlined by the respondents from both larger and smaller consultancies would follow that the previous situation. They would be provided keywords which would be used for semiotic analysis .This would lead to concept generation to capture the meaning in form.

5.3 Integration of end users in development of brand languages

Question 4- *"How important is it to involve target users (through interviews/focus groups) in the development of a brand language?"*

In general, the opinion of the respondents was it is difficult to involve target users in the development of brand languages. Firstly, it was considered somebody not fully rehearsed in 'design-speak' would not understand it. Secondly, client confidentiality needs to be maintained, and bringing in outside users at this phase of the project could jeopardise it. Respondent B did explain that target users had been involved previously, but at a much later stage in the development in order to gauge the emotional responses to certain colour choices and material finishes. This can however be considered an anomaly for this study.

6.0 Discussion

6.1 Introduction

This section will discuss the findings of the literature review and the empirical research. The literature will be compared against the findings from the interviews to establish its validity. The comparisons will be made on the following questions:

- How do products trigger an emotional response from users?
- How do people become attached to branded objects?
- What tools are used by designers to articulate the values of a brand through design?

6.2 Methodology Review

The methodology was undertaken successfully in the given time. The required information relating to the study was gathered and successfully analysed.

The telephone interviews with designers were successful in eliciting the required information. The interviews were planned to last approximately fifteen minutes. However, all five of them lasted for at least twenty, with two respondents talking for roughly thirty minutes. This allowed for greater depth and understanding of the techniques employed by designers. The two longer interviews did not bias the results by being longer in duration as a consensus view was still found. The longer time simply allowed the designers to articulate their answers clearly to aid understanding.

The case studies were completed successfully. However, finding the literature required was not as simple as anticipated and was fairly time consuming.

The interviews with users were largely completed successfully. It was noted in the interviews that participants D and E did not seem particularly interested in the subject and needed prompting and tact from the interviewer to elicit the information. The task to complete a 'brand board' was completed successfully by the younger participants in the sample population. The two older members were unable to offer the same quality of information. A single picture of their current mobile phone was stuck down by participant E with no further comment on their perception of the brand. Respondent F failed to complete the task, which did not consequently impair the results severely as the participant was communicative in the interview and was able to articulate their answers clearly without the assistance of the board.

6.3 Emotional Responses to Branded Products

The literature review highlighted that people tend to respond to products on two levels of cognitive processing. First, the product in use, and second, emotional interpretation. The concept of emotional interpretation presented by Norman (2004) and Khaslavsky (1999) suggested users acquire objects which share the same values as them in order to reflect a desired image. These findings were considered rather general and were not were not able to identify if this would work the same for branded items. As expected, the empirical investigations undertaken were able to confirm that this link also existed when considering branded objects establishing that users acquire objects produced by brands which have values the users aspire to.

The interviews also highlighted that the reflected image communicated by products was significant; however, the brand of the product was not shown to be a critical part of this. Surprisingly, the display of a damaged phone was conceded by two respondents as a show of indifference and nonchalance, communicating an 'I don't care' attitude. It should be highlighted here these were the two younger respondents in the population sample and not a consensus view. The damage can be seen as an acquired feature of the phone which conveniently acts as a vehicle to present a subversive attitude and image, much in the same way people wear ripped jeans.

Although this finding is not a result of branding, it presents an opportunity which brands could harness to provide users a greater sense of ownership, acting as a further platform for brands to accommodate the values of users.

6.3 Emotional attachment to branded products

Previous studies by Csikszentmihalyi (1981) suggested emotional attachment to objects was likely to occur if they were linked to memories. Csikszentmihalyi was unable to offer suggestion as to how branding has an influence on this. The empirical investigation found past associations were directly linked to brands, but surprisingly not branded objects. Three of the respondents had returned to the same brand for the third time, citing familiar experiences to those they experienced years before with the same brand as the deciding factors. It is interesting to note Csikszentmihalyi's model for attachment is not exclusive to physical items, but for the metaphysical concept of brands too.

The theory presented by Csikszentmihalyi was however discovered to have significance with physical items too. Unexpectedly however, the respondents were unanimous in commenting that the prospect of losing the phone was not particularly worrying, but damaging it was. Aside from enhancing the reflected image of the user as discussed previously, the idea of a damaged object provoking emotional attachment relates to the previous literature in two further ways. As Chapman (2005) suggested when discussing the success of the Tamagotchi, users have a primal urge to nurture, which elevates the human-object engagement. Damage to a phone may provoke an emotional response from users which prompts them to relate to their phone on a more significant level and take responsibility for it. The idea of memory and association presented by Csikszentmihalyi could also rationalise this finding, with the actual event of damaging the phone being remembered each time it is used.

It may be considered that these two themes of brand and product are still considered disparate, and when emotional attachment to branded products does occur it can not be dictated by the brand, such as unpredictable damage. Products may therefore be considered to act as temporary vehicles of engagement between the brand and the user, acting simply as a conduit for the emotional relationship.

6.4 Methods for communicating brand through products

Product Semantics methodology was shown in the literature review as the foremost method of translating a brand's values into 3D form. These methods were theorised chiefly by academics from universities and were not gathered from practising industrial designers. No mention of the term 'product semantics' was made during the interviews with designers, although the underlying theory was similar.

The framework proposed in the literature was split into two main sections; analysis and translation. Analysis involved splitting a brand's values into explicit and implicit visual cues. The consensus approach from the interviews suggested that no significant stage of splitting the product into visual cues was undertaken. Keywords of what the brand wishes to say would instead be given to the designers from the client's marketing team.

Karjalainen (2007) suggests the implicit cues, which are the deeper philosophical associations people have with brands should be applied liberally. Similarly, central to the methods used by designers was the concept of semiotics .Semiotic analysis requires the identification of the cultural significance of the keywords. These two concepts are similar in their approach as they stress the importance of the subtle, less tangible associations people have with objects. The designers suggested these meanings are later used to drive an image search of reference material to inform a design. No method of such application however was suggested in the literature.

The interviews and the literature highlighted that it is not possible to apply the obvious visual traits of a brand over every product as scale and appropriateness of the product require different approaches. Participant B suggested this was more common in car design as the scale is larger, and differences in subtleties of curve and form are more obvious if they change between cars. Interestingly, Karjalainen (2007) used the example of a Volvo to describe the application of these explicit cues.

The methodologies outlined by Karjalainen (2007) and Warrel (2001) did not comment on how their approaches would alter in differing circumstances. The designers commented no change in approach would occur between designing a new visual language for an established brand and designing a new visual language for an emerging brand. Both would operate around the keywords provided. Designing products to fit into an existing range was the exception, as brand guidelines for the existing range would be provided requiring no prior semiotic analysis. Surprisingly, the interviews suggested that user involvement was highly limited during the development of brand languages. Athanakar (2001) suggested a more predictable outcome would occur if user input was considered at each stage of its development. The designers were comprehensive in suggesting that prospective users would not understand it. Furthermore, they outlined client confidentiality was critical and involving external parties could jeopardise this. It would have been interesting to establish this link clearly, as it is ultimately the users' response to the brand language proposed which is how a brand can influence the emotional state of their user through their products.

7.0 Conclusions

Although highly disputed, the definition of a brand may be considered to be a consistent emotional response to a company over a period of time. Names and logos are not significant, rather, it is the associations and experiences customers have with a company.

7.1 How a company's branding strategy and product design relate to each other

Product design can be considered one of many equal elements in communicating a brand. The significance of design above other elements is argued by designers but disputed by marketers, although successful example of brands has been those which focus strongly on design. It is agreed however that all elements of a brand's output should share the same vision and carry the same message. Successful brands are those with clarity for what they stand for who deliver the same offer consistently.

7.2 How branded products can evoke emotion

Products which emotionally appeal to users are those which help to establish their identity, as users acquire products from brands which share the same values as the user has or aspires to. The image communicated by a product is an important aspect of self actualisation, but has been shown not be exclusive to branded objects.

7.3 The methodology employed by designers to communicate a brand's values through product design

Designers are given keywords from marketers which reflect the values of the brand. These keywords are used to conduct a phase of semiotic analysis. Semiotics in this respect concern the investigation into the cultural and associative meanings attached to a keyword in its context, which is dependent on the user and the market. Imagery which is able to communicate the desired semiotic meaning is collated to inform the visual design process. Users are generally not involved in the process as this would impair client confidentiality and are considered unable to grasp stages of designing a brand language.

7.3.1 How people become attached to branded products

People become attached to brands through memory, familiarity and association. This is the same way in which people become attached to non branded items such as furniture and photographs. The branded product has not been shown to be significant in isolation, but acts as a device to for the brand to connect to the user to create association and build memories of the experiences shared between them. Damage to products has been shown to provoke a sense of responsibility and nurture which promotes a deeper human-object relationship, although this is irrespective of influence from the brand.

7.4 Research Limitations

Although a large spread of participants over a range of ages were selected in accordance to recommendations in the literature, it should be remembered that the population sampled for the user investigations may not be fully reflective of the views of the wider population.

Similarly, the results yielded from the designers may not be adherent to the entire UK or international consensus of methodologies employed by designers. These shortcomings in the research were due to time restrictions.

7.5 Further Study

Interviewing a larger number of participants would achieve a better representation of the wider population. Investigating users connections to cars (as these were outlined with mobile phones as an emotional branded product) would act as comparison against the findings generated in this study.

A further avenue of investigation could identify if nurture and personalisation were viable options for brands to exploit in the design of their products. It would be interesting to conduct a 'concept design' project to trial adventurous product concepts which may successfully promote nurture and personalisation in their design and compare the findings against those established in this study.

8.0 Bibliography

Aakar, A 2001. Brand Leadership. London: Free Press.

Aakar, A 2002. Building Strong Brands. London: Free Press.

Barthes, R 1992. Mythologies. London: Vintage

Butler J, *et al,*2003. Universal Principles of Design. Gloucester, MA: Rockport

Cobley P, 2004. Introducing Semiotics. London: Icon Books Ltd

Kelly T, 2001. The Art of Innovation, London : Profile Books

Kelly T, 2005. The Ten Faces of Innovation, Doubleday: New York

Norman, D, 2002. The Design of Everyday things 3rd ed, New York: Basic Books

9.0 References

Anon, 2009. Pressing Needs (online) Available at:
> http://standingoncommonground.org/images/maslows_hierarchy.gif (accessed 4 December 2008)

Apple, 2009. Apple Values (online) Available at: http://www.apple.com/uk/pr/ (accessed 4 December 2008)

Athavankar, U., 1990 . The Semantic Profile of Products – An Approach to Product Semantics Based on Strategies Used in Human Information Processing. Semantic Vision in Design 2nd ed , Helsinki : UIAH Press.

Blaich, R 1989. Forms of Design. In: University of Industrial Arts Helsinki. Product Semantics '89 Conference, 25 March 1989. Helsinki. The Finnish Government Printing Centre, Helsinki

Burnette, C 1992. cited in Ganz, 1992: 180) Innovation Michigan: Industrial Designers Society of America

Chapman, J 2005. Emotionally Durable Design- Objects, Experiences & Empathy. London: Earthscan.

Christou, C., 2009   Product Matters. *New Design,* April 2009. P48

Csikszentmihalyi, M., 1981. The Meaning of Things 2nd ed, Cambridge: Cambridge University Press

Davies, F 2009 Let get digital! (online) Available at:
> http://www.letsgodigital.org/en/21745/apple-mac-pro/&usg (accessed 4 December 2008)

Denscombe, M, 2001. The Good Research Guide 4th ed, Maidenhead: Open University Press

Design Council, 2008, The Value of Design (online) Available at:
http://www.designcouncil.org.uk/en/About-Design/Research/Value-of-Design-Factfinder/ (Accessed 1st January 2009)

Fiell , 2008, Design Now! Hong Kong: Taschen

GreenfieldBelser, 2008 What is a brand (online) Available at :
http://www.gbltd.com/big_ideas/?NewsID=32 (accessed 4 December 2008)

Grinyer, C, 2008. Digital Design (online) Available at:
http://www.clivegrinyer.com/articles.html (Accessed 12th December 2008)

Gobe, M, 2001. Emotional Branding, The new paradigm for connecting brands to people New York: Allworth Press

Heckert , 2000 in McDonagh, D et al Design and Emotion :The experience of everyday things London: Taylor and Francis

Hill, D, 2005, Getting Emotional with Dan Hill (online) Available at http://www.design-emotion.com/2008/06/29/getting-emotional-with-dan-hill/ (Accessed 4 December 2008)

Interbrand, 2008, Best Global Brands (online)
http://www.interbrand.com/best_global_brands.aspx (Accessed 2nd January 2009)

Kapferer, J., 2008. The New Strategic Brand Management, Creating and sustaining brand equity long term. 4th ed, London: Kogan Page

Karjalainen, T, 2004, Semantic Transformations in Design, communicating strategic brand identity through product references , Helsinki: University of the Arts, Helsinki

Karjalainen, T, 2004. Design Communication ,in: Report and selected papers from the 3rd Nordcode Seminar & Workshop hosted by the Technical University of Denmark, (online) Available at: www.tolk.su.se/past_jan-jun_2006.html

Keller, K, 2005, Measuring Brand Equity. In Grover et al, ed. The Handbook of Market Research, Page 546- 569,

Khaslavsky, J,1999. Understanding the seductive experience, Communications of the ACM , 45(5) pp 4-49

Krippendorf, K 1989. Product Semantics; A triangulation and four design theories. In Vakeva, ed. Product Semantics '89, Page 3-23

Laver, G 2001 The underlying structure of brand awareness scores, Marketing Science,14(3) pp170-79

Lindstrom, M. 2005.,, Brand Sense London: Kogan Page

Marketing Week, 2009 Cultivating a responsible image (online) Available at: http://www.marketingweek.co.uk/cgi-bin/item.cgi?id=61820&u=pg_dtl_art_news&m=pg_hdr_art (Accessed 9 December 2008)

Maslow, A, 1999. Towards a psychology of being,3rd ed, Ohio: J.Wiley and Sons

Motorola 2009, About Motorola (online) Available at: http://www.motorola.com/content.jsp?globalObjectId=451-843 (Accessed 9 December 2008)

Neumeier, M, 2008, The Brand Gap Boston: New Riders

Nokia, 2009. Nokia way and values (online) Available at: http://www.nokia.com/A4126303
(Accessed 9 December 2008)

Norman, D, 2004. Emotional Design: Why we love or hate everyday things 3rd ed, New York:
Net Library

Ollins, W, 2003. Wally Ollins on brand London: Thames and Hudson

Panzer,K, 2000, Emotional marketing New York: Net Library

Philips Coorporate Design,2009. Philips Design-Our Approach (online) Available at:
http://www.design.philips.com/about/design/aboutus/approach/index.page (Accessed
16th January 2009)

Rich, H ,2008. Using design to pick stocks? (online) Available at:
http://www.businessweek.com/innovate/content/oct2005/id20051012_933081.htm
(Accessed 4th January 2009)

Robson, C ,2008. Real World Research.2nd ed, Oxford: Blackwell Publishing

Schmitt et al, 1997. Marketing Aesthetics, New York: The Free Press

Seymour, R , 2008. Embodying the essence of a brand (online) Available at:
http://www.seymourpowell.com/#/case_studies/13/ (Accessed 9 December 2008)

SonyEricsson, 2009, Behind the Name- Vision and Passion (online) Available at:
http://www.sonyericsson.com/cws/corporate/company/jobsandcareers/behindthename
(Accessed 14 February 2009)

Syarief et al, 2004. Evaluating the Semantic Approach through Horst Rittel's Second Generation
System Analysis (online) School of Science and Technology Chiba University,
Available at :

www.idemployee.id.tue.nl/g.w.m.rauterberg/conferences/CD_doNotOpen/ADC/final_paper

Swatch 2009. Official UK online Store (online) Available at: http://eu-shop.swatch.com/eshop/uk/en/Watches/Originals/Gent/GB743.aspx (Accessed 16th January 2009)

Strange Harvest 2009, Lemon Squeezy: Design tendencies after the juicy salif (online) Available at: http://www.strangeharvest.com/mt/archive/the_harvest/lemon_squeezy_design.php (Accessed 16th January 2009)

Sweet, F 1999. Frog-Form Follows Emotion . Boston : Watson-Guptill Publications

Warell, A ,2003, Towards a theory based method for evaluation of visual form syntactics (online) Chalmers School of technology, Available at: www.idemployee.id.tue.nl/g.w.m.rauterberg/conferences/CD_doNotOpen/ADC/final_paper

10.0 Appendices

Appendix A- Discussion guide for interviews with users

1.0 Priorities

What is the best thing about mobile phones?

What is the worst thing about mobile phones?

What are your three priorities when choosing a mobile phone

2.0 Relationship with brands

What brands of mobile phone have you had?

Which (of the above) would you be willing to try again and why?

Which ones would you not try again and why?

Of the following brands, which would you be willing to try?

-Nokia

-Samsung

-Sony Ericsson

-Motorola

-Apple

-LG

-Blackberry

-Sagem

-Alcatel

-HTC

Would you be willing to try other products by these brands?

3.0 Relationship with object (mobile phone)

What is the make and model of your current mobile phone?

How long have you had this phone?

Could you describe it to me as someone who has never seen it? (note- keywords they use to describe it)

What do you like most about the phone and which (colour, shape, specific functions- note relationships between this and priorities from mobiles)

Is there anything you dislike about this phone and why?

What made you choose this phone?

Have you had any other products by this brand before?- If yes, which ones, and what was your experience?

Would you choose this brand for a mobile phone again? Please provide a rationale for your answer

Would you buy other products from this brand?-If yes, identify which products and why. If no, why not?

3.1 Brand Board

Ask them to explain the imagery in as much detail as possible and why?

Ask them to explain how the brand makes them feel?

If the brand was a person, or type of person, who would it be?

What was your first encounter with the brand?

Would you buy products from this brand again?

Appendix B- Discussion Guide for Interview with Designers

- A well established brand wishes for you to aesthetically redesign n x product for them to fit in with their existing range. Can you briefly outline the methodology used to apply their brand traits on this product?

- A well established brand wishes to progress/develop their existing brand language and apply it to a new product or range of products. Can you briefly outline the methodology used?

- 3-A new company with no particular brand language wishes for you to aesthetically (re)design x product for them. Can you outline the methodology used to establish their values in 3 dimensions?

- 4-How important is it to involve target users (through interviews/focus groups) in the development of a brand language?

Appendix C- Brand Boards

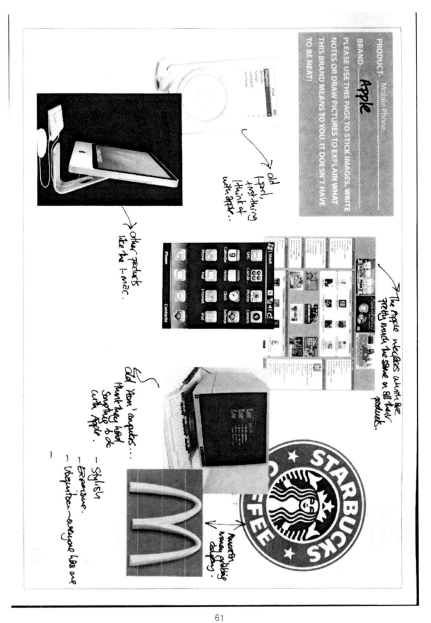

PRODUCT- Mobile Phone......

BRAND- **Apple**

PLEASE USE THIS PAGE TO STICK IMAGES, WRITE NOTES OR DRAW PICTURES TO EXPLAIN WHAT THIS BRAND MEANS TO YOU. IT DOESN'T HAVE TO BE NEAT!

→ old iPod, +nothing I think of with Apple...

→ other products like the I-mac.

The Apple interfaces are all pretty much the same on all their products.

Old Macs' computers... I think they had something to do with Apple.

- Stylish
- Expensive.
- Ubiquitous—everyone has one

Adverts, really selling lifestyle.

PRODUCT... Mobile Phone...

BRAND...

NOKIA

PLEASE USE THIS PAGE TO STICK IMAGES, WRITE
NOTES OR DRAW PICTURES TO EXPLAIN WHAT
THIS BRAND MEANS TO YOU. IT DOESN'T HAVE
TO BE NEAT!

RELIABLE

The 'STANDARD' PHONE   ~ EVERYONE USED TO HAVE THE NOKIA 3310

- NOT AS FLASHY

- THE LONDON PHONE

ONE OF THE ORIGINAL(?)

Always go for cheapest Nokia phone
Use until it breaks.

Never had any phone
which isn't a Nokia

THESE
FOR AN
EMERGENCY!

USUAL MONEY GRABBING COMPANY

('CONNECTING
PEOPLE')

- KEY COMPONENT
(IN COMMUNICATION

SCARY LIKE
ALL PHONE
BRANDS

PRODUCT: Mobile Phone

BRAND: NoKIA

PLEASE USE THIS PAGE TO STICK IMAGES, WRITE NOTES OR DRAW PICTURES TO EXPLAIN WHAT THIS BRAND MEANS TO YOU. IT DOESN'T HAVE TO BE NEAT.

THE OLD GLOW CHANCING COVERS

↳ BRICK SHAPES, BRICK PHONES.
— RELIABLE
— BASIC

— EVERYONE AT SCHOOL HAD IT BECAUSE OF SNAKE.
— PHONE EVERYONE HAS.

↳ IKEA, SKANDINAVIAN STYLE

PRODUCT: Mobile Phone...

BRAND: Nokia

PLEASE USE THIS PAGE TO STICK IMAGES, WRITE NOTES OR DRAW PICTURES TO EXPLAIN WHAT THIS BRAND MEANS TO YOU. IT DOESN'T HAVE TO BE NEAT!

→ Current phone.
Nokia's had notes,
very reliable, not
expensive. Good quality
at the right price.

→ Always reminded of before
wilderness, always where you
never get chance and
started using them for work.

— Daughters had this phone first. Liked the look and feel (as it would fit easily into pocket and handbag.

— Motorola makes me want ginger.

MOTOROLA

Appendix D-Interview with users transcripts

Transcription of user interview 1

Interviewer-What do you think the best thing is about mobile phones?

Participant A- Probably the connectivity, I like being in touch with people when I want to be......I've had phones for so long it would be weird not having that connectivity now...

Interviewer- So do you find that connectivity is an important thing for you now?

Participant A-Yeah, I guess so, I've had phones since I was 14 so I'm used to having it there.

Interviewer-What do you think the worst thing about mobile phones are then?

Participant A-Probably the health risks, the long term health risks, I've heard it damages your sperm count and gives you brain tumours..not sure if that is true but it's a bit of a worry. Also charging it, fucking hate charging it. There is nothing worse than having to find a charger or wait for it to charge.

Interviewer-What are your three priorities when choosing a mobile phone?

Participant A- User Interface is a big one, I really hate it when you have a bad interface. I had a Sony ericsson a couple of years ago, it was quite a cool looking phone, but the thing that I really liked about it was that it had a really cool interface, this really cool scroll wheel thing which you could use on games as well, and it was the first time I had seen something like that, on a phone, so that kind of stuck in my mind. I went and got one myself, sorry, I should have said that it was my mates' first, but yeah, got one myself and I really liked it.

Interviewer-Have you had another Sony ericsson since?

Participant A-Yeah, two more, I think, cos I just really liked the interface on it. I had a huge brick of a Nokia before then, it just wasn't as good so I haven't gone back to them since.

Interviewer-What other things are important for you when buying a phone?

Participant A-Deals obviously, if there is a good deal on that might influence it.....dunno, the look I suppose. And also whatever comes free with it.

Interviewer- Can you elaborate on what you said earlier about not liking Nokias?

Participant A-I dunno, they're just big and chunky, the one I had one and I've played with a few of my mate's since and they're the same. They don't really feel that nice to use...

66

Interviewer-Why aren't they nice to use?

Participant A- They just feel chunky……I can remember the screen broke on mine too, I kept it for a while afterwards as I liked the phone, but when I got rid of it when I got my Sony ericsson it just looked really brick like. I've had to use it a couple of times since and it just seems a bit clunky.

Interviewer- Why did you keep it when the screen broke?

Participant A- Because I couldn't afford a new one!

Interviewer- Would you go back to Nokia?

Participant A-Not sure, I think they have a crap user interface which is not what I want. The one I had was one of those ones with a colour screen when colour screens first came out, it looked pretty shit, I thought so at the time even though it was supposed to be this new technology. And the screen was about an inch away from the top of the phone. When I got my I-phone though, the other phone I was going to get was a Nokia, like Nokia's version of the I-Phone. I think I would definitely consider other brands first..

Interviewer- Do you think this depends on a phone to phone basis, or are you loyal to a brand?

Participant A- I'm not sure, as I said, I really liked the SonyEricsson I had so I went back to them, but both the phones they did were pretty cool looking and I liked their features. The reason I didn't go back to Nokia when I got my I-phone was because it wasn't nice to use, I really liked the look of it though, but it felt a bit shit in my hand and a bit tiresome to use.

Interviewer- I'm going to list a few mobile phone brands, and you have to tell me if you are willing to try them, and what you associate with them, ok?!

Participant A-Yep

Interviewer- OK, Nokia!

Participant A-Ha ha, ok. Well as I said, I find them a bit chunky, I might try them again. I just think of Volvos for some reason when I think of Nokia's, ha ha, and that old advert where the woman was changing covers, you know , the changeable covers, and she was moving them down the washing line. I think the styling of their products is a bit blocky too, not very slick, and everyone seems to have them. They're a bit too, err, ubiquitous, I don't think anyone is special or different if they have a Nokia..

Interviewer- You find them a bit too widespread?

Participant A- yeah, I mean, I've got an I-phone, and I know everyone has I-pods these days, but they seem a bit more special, but Nokia's ARE mobile phones if that makes sense, just the standard mobile phone.

Interviewer- Ok, Samsung..

Participant A- Yeah I quite like Samsungs stuff. I really liked their tellys, they look pretty cool, I can't say I can remember what any of their phones look like though. But if I saw one of their phones I liked I don't think there would be any reason why I wouldn't want it.

Interviewer- So would you buy one of their TVs?

Participant A- Yeah, why not, they look pretty cool, I like the black on them, its really slick and classy looking.

Interviewer- Is that something you associate with Samsung, slick looks, impressive styling?

Participant A-Yeah, they do some nice stuff.

Interviewer- Is that something which is important to you, looks?

Participant A- Err, not so much as usability and how it feels to use, but yeah I suppose it is.

Interviewer- What else do you associate with Samsung?

Participant A- Blue...Shiny black, I'm not sure. That little blue light they all seem to have, it's the same as on the logo.

Interviewer-Ok, LG?

Participant A- I can't really say I know what their phones look like....I know their TVs looks nice, with that little red ring on the bottom.

Interviewer- You can't think of any of their phones? What they look like?

Participant A-No, sorry! If they looked like their TVs that would be good. But I've never had or used an LG product before so I can't think what they would be like.

Interviewer- What do you associate with LG?

Participant A- Shiny black again, but a bit fatter. Quite similar to Samsung aren't they? I think of posh Japanese businessmen or something, very hi tech, Asian...

Interviewer- Sony, well, Sonyerricson?

Participant A- Yeah, I would definitely get more Sony stuff, and Sonyericcson phones. They were really cool to use and I would go back to them.

Interviewer- What do you associate with Sonyerrcison?

Participant A- Orange, not the phone company, but the colour. That kind of soft feel orange they have on their phones. Any silver or shinyness. Their phones are a bit bling compared to other mobiles.

Interviewer- Can you think why that is?

Participant A- Um, I dunno, I think they are aimed at teenagers because I had mine when I was a teenager, they are quite flashy and 'look at me', I'm not sure If I've grown out of that now.

Interviewer- Sagem?

Participant A- Sagem?! Never heard of them..can't think of anything there!

Interviewer- OK, BenQ?

Participant A- BenQ? Ha ha, again, never heard of them either!

Interviewer- OK, Grundig?

Participant A- Don't they make radios not phones?

Interviewer- Yes they do..

Participant A- I don't think I'd buy one of theirs. Not very trendy is it Grundig . Sounds like guinea pig.

Interviewer- Ok, lets talk about your current mobile phone. What is the make and model of your current phone?

Participant A- Ok, its an Apple I-phone

Interviewer-How long have you had this phone?

Participant A-About a year

Interviewer- Could you describe it to me as someone who has never seen it?

Participant A- Ok, well, its black, glossy, about the size of your hand, its quite solid and sturdy, feels well built. Touch screen interface, it seems to only really do stuff when its on…

Interviewer-What do you like most about the phone?

Participant A-Definitely the interface, feels really nice to use, it's a bit plain without it being switched on. I like the fact it is always on the internet, you can be on it anytime. I like the fact its only got one button, which acts as the menu button, so you never get lost.

Interviewer- How does that make you feel?

Participant A- Its pretty reassuring, its got loads of these functions but having that there is like a comfort.

Interviewer- Is there anything you dislike about the phone?

Participant A- yes, I don't really like how it syncs to the computer when ever you want to charge it, that's a ball ache. I think Apple are a bit greedy too because after it synced with my compute once, I lost all my applications, and I had to pay for them again. I thought they would know that I'd already paid for the ones I had, but I think they did that deliberately.

Interviewer- Do you trust Apple as a brand?

Participant A- yeah, but they are a super corporate, like Starbucks or McDonalds, I'm not sure if I am so keen on that.

Interviewer-Is there anything else you dislike about Apple as a brand?

Participant A- Yeah, all their stuff is really expensive

Interviewer- Have you got any other Apple products?

Participant A- Nope

Interviewer- Is that because they are expensive?

Participant A- To be honest, yeah. Its quality stuff, but I think it is disproportionately expensive. I paid more for the I-phone because I think its pretty impressive for the price.

Interviewer- What do you associate with Apple then?

Participant A- Its all shiny, robust. All the software is really robust, it doesn't crash as much as windows.

Interviewer- Is what's going on inside important to you as well?

Participant A- yeah, because that's what a phone is really, the inside, the interface.

Interviewer- Would you have another I-phone again?

Participant A- yeah, probably

Interviewer-Why?

Participant A- I found it to be quite a good phone, its solid, shiny, and the interface and software is great.

Interviewer-Would you buy other products from this brand?

Participant A- yeah, I would really like a Mac book, they're head and shoulders above the rest. The visibility on them is great and you can have them on your lap because thy vent properly.

Interviewer- How would you feel if you lost it?

Participant A-Sick!!

Interviewer- Can you elaborate on why?

Participant A- I think...I think its because I spent so long looking after it, and not getting it scratched, that if it went , it was like time wasted.

Interviewer- So you feel like you invested a lot of time and care with it?

Participant A- yeah, definitely, and because it's a desirable and expensive thing, I would feel ashamed. Its got a huge crack on it actually on the back, which I feel a bit upset about, but I don't want another one as it wouldn't feel like my phone. It would feel like cheating if I got a new one!

Transcription of user interview 2

Interviewer-What do you think is the best thing about mobile phones?

Participant B- Connectivity, definitely, I like being in touch with my family whenever I want, I find that really important. I like having it with me when I go running, and I probably go later on in the evening than I would otherwise because I know it is there.

Interviewer- So, do you find having a phone on you comforting, reassuring?

Participant B- Yes, definitively. I like knowing it is there, I like having the option to be in contact when I need it

Interviewer- And the worst thing about them?

Participant B-Probably the fact you have to charge it when its dead. I know that sounds stupid, but it is a bit of a hassle having to anchor it down and keep it fixed when you charge it. It is no longer mobile, you see. Also, I don't like on other phones, not this one, how they can ring in your handbag when you are not aware, suddenly you can run up a huge bill.

Interviewer- What would you say your three priorities are when choosing a phone?

Participant B-Definitely having it like a flip phone, or clamshell design, because then it won't go off in my handbag. Its quite embarrassing if you ring somebody for a few minutes or leave and answer phone message for ages when you aren't actually talking.

Interviewer-OK, what other priorities do you have? What influences your purchase decisions?

Participant B- Usually if there is a good deal on, that would help. This phone is actually on a contract from Tesco, which I know isn't terribly trendy or glamorous, but the phone is the same as if it were on Orange or O2, so I don't think it matters particularly.

Interviewer- If Tesco did handsets, would you have one of those?

Participant B- No, definitely not, you don't really want to advertise that do you!

Interviewer- Why not?

Participant B- Well, its Tesco isn't it, it would seem a bit cheap (laughs)

Interviewer- Which brands of handset have you had then?

Participant B- Motorola, which is my current one, and Nokia, I've only had two.

Interviewer- Would you be willing to have Motorola again?

Participant B- I suppose so, depends if I like that actual phone. I bought this one without really noticing it was a Motorola until I had it.

Interviewer-So it was the phone itself you were drawn to...not so much the brand?

Participant B- Yes

Interviewer- OK, do you like the Motorola brand now after your experience with that phone?

Participant B- Yes, because I've noticed it more now I'm aware that it's the phone I've got, I've started to think its actually quite a nice make.

Interviewer- What do you think makes it nice?

Participant B- I'm not sure, I think they are rather stylish and well built.

Interviewer- Ok, what was it about Nokia which you were drawn to?

Participant B- Well, my husband had Nokias for a long time as he used them with work, and I suppose it was the brand which I was most familiar with because of that. I think because he had had them for years I always thought they must be pretty good so I went and bought one.

Interviewer- Do you see them as reliable phones?

Participant B- Yes........and no (laughs)

Interviewer- Can you elaborate on that at all?

Participant B- Well, they seem to work really well, but the screen on mine broke and I had to keep a bit of sellotape on it to keep it together.

Interviewer- How long was it until you actually changed it?

Participant B- I suppose it would be about six months! I know that's bad, but I didn't really want to change it, it still worked and I wasn't too bothered about the tape.

Interviewer- You didn't feel you might have looked a bit cheap or anything?!

Participant B- No,I don't think anyone notices, I don't think anyone is really that bothered by it!

Interviewer- So, to clarify, you replaced it with the Motorola as it was on offer at Tesco?

Participant B- yes, it was a good deal, and one of my daughters had one of those Razor phones which I thought was fairly attractive so I decided to buy one too!

Interviewer- What is it about that phone which you find attractive?

Participant B- I'm not sure, I mean, to look at, its nice and shiny, with metal looking bits on it. But its got a nice weight to it

Interviewer- Was that noticed when you looked at your daughter's phone?

Participant B- Yes I suppose it would have been

Interviewer-Ok, I'm going to read you a list of Mobile phone brands, and you have to tell me which ones you are willing to try.

Participant B- Ok

Interviewer- Nokia

Participant B- Well, its fairly widespread isn't it. Yes I would be willing to have another one of theirs

Interviewer-What do you associate with Nokias?

Participant B- Well, I always think of my husbands old telephone which I used to borrow to make calls on if we were on holiday or abroad.

Interviewer- Samsung?

Participant B- I don't really know much about Samsung if I'm perfectly honest. I think the small television we have in the kitchen might be a Samsung…..(*NB. It is actually a Sony*) I'm not sure to be perfectly honest. I can't actually think of anything Samsung….

Interviewer- Do you have any associations with Samsung then?

Participant B- As I said, I can't think of anything they have done I'm afraid!

Interviewer- Ok, next one, LG?

Participant B- (laughs) Again, I can't think of anything they have done! Did they do the pebble phone?

Interviewer- That was Motorola as well

Participant B- Was it really? Ok, well, can we do Motorolla?

Interviewer- Yes

Participant B- Well, I think they have fairly stylish phones, I remember that pebble phone, and I have the Razor. They all have such exciting names don't they!

Interviewer- Do you think Motorola is an exciting brand?

Participant B-Not really, I think they might be now though. When I was a girl, we used to have a Motorola radio at my parents' house, which was this great big thing with wood on it. Motorola was considered a fairly cheap brand back then, it was when my parents didn't have too much money I think and it was what we could afford.

Interviewer- Ok, Sony Ericcson?

Participant B- I can't say I have heard of them…I have heard of Sony, but I can't think of anything that Sony Ericston have done.

Interviewer- OK, next one, Apple?

Participant B- As in I-pods, and computers?

Interviewer- Yes

Participant B- Do they do I-pod phones too?

Interviewer- Yes

Participant B- Really, I haven't seen those. Ok, well, we had an Apple Macintosh a few years ago, we had it for ages, far too long I think. My daughters used to tell us to replace it with a new one. It had this great orange screen. I can remember it was nice to use, it was fairly pretty.

Interviewer- Would you have an I-phone if it was as good as the Macintosh computer you had?

Participant B- Yes, I suppose I would, it would last a long time.

Interviewer, ok- Blackberry?

Participant B- Oh no, wouldn't want one of those!

Interviewer- Why not?

Participant B- Well, my other daughter has one, she is always on it sending emails, I don't think its healthy emailing that often.

Interviewer- Ok, HTC?

Participant B- Sorry, not heard of them…

Interviewer- Alcatel?

Participant B- (blank expression) Nope! Sorry

Interviewer- BenQ?

Participant B- Never heard of them either I'm afraid!

Interviewer- Ok, lets discuss your current phone. How long have you had your Motorola Razr?

Participant B- About a year

Interviewer- Could you describe it to me as someone who has never seen it?

Participant B-Well, its squarish, shiny, its quite cold to touch. Its got a good weight to it….I like that. It's a flip phone, which is good as it doesn't go off, its got a black screen…that's about it really!

Interviewer- What is it that you like the most about the phone?

Participant B- Well, the fact it is a flip phone. And the weight of it.

Interviewer-Is there anything you dislike about the phone?

Participant B- No not really, its quite nice.

Transcription of user interview 3

Interviewer- What do you think the best thing about having a mobile phone is?

Participant C- It's good when you're younger because your parents will let you go out, for me, I find the connectivity pretty essential. I don't use all the extra functions or anything like that. I like having that link all the time.

Interviewer- Do you think it's a comfort thing having that there?

Participant C- yeah kind of, I'm not as bad as some people who will get really paniky if they don't have their phone with them. I tend to leave it places and walk away. I don't like it. I don't like how everyone has become dependant on them. I spent the whole summer in America, didn't switch it on once.

Interviewer- Is that the worst thing about them then?

Participant C- Yeah, I don't like how you can be contacted at all times.

Interviewer- Isn't that contradicting what you just said?

Participant C- Yeah, that's the reason I have it, for emergencies, so that I can get in contact with people in emergencies, but I don't like how they can get in contact with me. If that makes sense!

Interviewer- What are your three priorities when choosing a phone?

Participant C- Cost, reliability, its got to be something that will just last for years. What I basically do is go for the cheapest Nokia every time, I've had three phones, I've only replaced them when they have been completely broken. I've never just updated them.

Interviewer- What brands have you had then?

Participant C- Nokia, Nokia, Nokia. Do you want me to explain why?

Interviewer- Yes please

Participant C- The first Nokia I had was the 3330. Do you remember everyone at school had the 3330? That was like the standard phone. On my mood board here, I've got Nokia as like the standard phone. Its like the basic building block of all phones. Because at the point I started to get phones, that's the one everyone had.

Interviewer- Do you see Nokia as just the standard then?

Participant C- Yeah. All the other ones are just like flashy versions of them. And in that way, I kind of see them as reliable. A few years later I broke, so I just went for its updated version, the

3310, I think that's what it was, I stuck with them on orange as I couldn't be arsed to update my number. And then I went for whichever one I've got at the moment, I think it's a 2610, which was the cheapest Nokia in the Orange shop. I've just always stuck with that because its reliable. It looks reliable too, even though that phone screen is crap, you can't see it when you're walking outside

Interviewer- Do you think that's because it's a cheap phone, they've cut corners?

Participant C- I don't know, I don't think it should be anymore expensive to sort that out.

Interviewer- Do you find anything annoying about that phone?

Participant C- The buttons are too close together, but if they are the standard shape, and this is the standard shape, then I should know which one is which.

Interviewer- Would you be willing to try other brands in the future?

Participant C- I'm not really fussed, I've never really been fussed.

Interviewer- So a phone for you is not about 'showiness'?

Participant C- Nah, I mean, look, I've selotaped the back on this one, because I've lost the back, its not about image. Well, actually, maybe it could be, maybe I'm making a statement about why I don't have a new one

Interviewer- Do you think that is conscious or subconscious you are doing that?

Participant C- Well, I think maybe I do show off a bit the fact that I don't have a back to it, so maybe it is a statement.

Interviewer- OK, like displaying you're laziness?

Participant C-Yeah, maybe.

Interviewer- Would you buy other products by Nokia?

Participant C- What other products do they do?

Interviewer- Headsets, hands free kits…

Participant C- Well that's just make your phone flashier so no

Interviewer- What if Nokia were to bring out, say, TVs, or stereos?

Participant C- I wouldn't be put off them, but I tend to see them as someone who specialises in phones, like I say, I consider Nokia the standard phone, I would go for somebody who I would consider the standard for TVs

Interviewer- How would you feel if you saw adverts for Nokia TVs though, would you feel a bit cheated or mislead?

Participant C- I wouldn't feel cheated, I'm not sure, I might like it if I got used to the idea, I just feel I'd question it, like, 'has that got something to do with a phone?' Saying that though, even though I associate Apple with computers, I still think their I-phone is of a decent quality.

Interviewer- How would you feel if Nokia were doing some internet based thing, or something to do with connectivity?

Participant C- Again, I wouldn't be put off, but I would still go with the brands who I see who specialise in that sort of thing. I still see them as purely a phone brand.

Interviewer- How long have you had that phone then?

Participant C- For about 2, 3 years.

Interviewer- Could you describe it to me as someone who has never seen it before?

Participant C- Ok, its kind of the standard shape of a phone, its just a black rectangle, it should have a back part, its got a matte kind of rubbery surface, and a kind of glossy surface, and a kind of appearing screen, if its not active, you can't really differentiate the screen from the rest of it.

Interviewer- What do you like about it?

Participant C- Its not fussy, its just got that practical look to it. It doesn't transform or fold out or anything. I find phones scary, but this one, I know what its doing, its just got a normal keypad, I don't want it overcomplicating it.

Interviewer-Can you clarify what made you choose that phone then?

Participant C- Price, brand, and company. I always go for cheapest Nokia, Orange, pay as you go. Never had any different. Had my first one when I was 14, even considered having a pager, because I didn't like the idea of having a phone, and my parents wanted to stay in touch.

Interviewer- If you were to lose that, not the numbers or sim card, how would you feel?

Participant C- I'm not sure, its quite nice feeling connected, I wouldn't like to be without it.

Interviewer- No, but that actual phone

Participant C- Um, I'd miss it a bit I suppose, I like the fact the back has gone, it feels a bit more like mine like that.

Interviewer- Where does it live most of the time?

Participant C- In my bag

Interviewer- Never in your pocket?

Participant C- No, in my bag

Interviewer- So you like the connectivity, but not the immediate connectivity?

Participant C- Yeah, I suppose I like it in the way that you have a house phone, its nice having it there but I don't want it in my face. I like how people can give me a missed call or leave a message though.

Brand Board

Interviewer- Ok, can you talk me through this then

Participant C- Ok, well, like I said, you've got that standard block, its not too flashy, however I have just seen somebody's new Nokia phone, which is the rival to the I-phone, which has got a little stick, which is quite cool. The look of it, and the feel of it, still has the boring Nokia look, even though it has flashy functions.

Interviewer- What do you think of that, the fact that I-phones are this lovely object?

Participant C- I-phones to me are more of a life organiser, my mum has one of them and uses it to get around London if she is lost. Just use you're a-z!

Interviewer- What do you think about Nokia doing it? Do you think tits copying Apple or anything?

Participant C- Well no everyone is copying everyone else anyway! Apple is a bit more glamorous anyway. Nokia's slogan is connecting people, I think that's what they're about, not fancy applications, just connecting people.

Interviewer- Do you think what they say about their brand, is true about what you think about them?

Participant C- yeah, definitely! But they are scary, phones.

Interviewer- Why do you find phones scary

Participant C- I'm not sure, even at home, or at work, I don't like answering the phone, I think its because you can't read people, you can't get to grips with what they are kind of saying properly, or the subtleties, and that kind of scares me in a way. I don't like intruding people, that's why I hate ringing up people. Also the fact technology, everything about technology is scary

Interviewer- Do you think the way that they deliver their technology is human or emotional?

Participant C- Er, not really, some of its still a bit scary. I think Nokia are perhaps a bit more user friendly than other ones.

Interviewer- What made you go for a Nokia in the first place?

Participant C- It was kind of the craze at the time!

Transcription of user interview 4

Interviewer- Can you describe your camera to me as someone who has never seen it before?

Participant D- OK, its quite big and chunky, its got a camera on the bag of it, its got a little joystick in the middle, loads of buttons and stuff on the side, it's a bit like a brick

Interviewer- What do you think the best thing is about mobile phones?

Participant D-I can give someone a quick ring, and someone can always contact me, its convenient

Interviewer- What's the worst thing about mobile phones?

Participant D- All the shit you get on it. Things like being contacted all the time don't bother me, but all the features which are on there are really inaccessible, I don't even know how to get onto my contacts list from this, and I've had it for two years. Its got a load of other stuff on it- world, gps, entertainment, I don't even know how to use it.

Interviewer-So what are your priorities when choosing a phone?

Participant D- Just to make calls, and maybe make a text.

Interviewer- What brands of mobile phone have you had?

Participant D- I've had two SonyEriccsons, one LG, Nokia, and I had a cheap crappy one, can't remember what brand it was, it was from Sainsburys.

Interviewer- Would you go back to those brands again?

Participant D- Well, they were all pretty shit because I don't go out and buy mobile phones, they get given to me, this was an old hand me down from a mate from work, my very first SonyEriccson was given to me by my parents when I was 13, my Nokia was a hand me down from my dad, my mum thought she was doing me a favour by getting me a flip phone, nice gesture, but it wasn't, so I've never actively gone out and bought a mobile phone.

Interviewer- Ok, lets start with LG first, would you be willing to buy LG products again, based on your experiences with that phone?

Participant D- Yeah, to be fair, the LG one was pParticipant Dably the best out of all of them, it was clean, there was no extra crap on it, I just remember the outside surface of it was really shiny and glossy, really nice, like this one has flappy things here, a load of buttons on the side, but this one didn't have any of that, it didn't have any of that, it just had a screen, some buttons, that was pretty much it.

Interviewer- Ok, if you were buying another one, would you go back to Nokia, based on your experiences with it before?

Participant D- Well, it's a bit hard to say, because it was a long time ago I had that Nokia, but I can remember really liking snake, the game

Interviewer- So was it games which attracted you to it?

Participant D- When I was younger it was

Interviewer- SonyErriccson?

Participant D- I would never have a SonyEriccson again, I hate the Sony brand, except Sony TVs

Interviewer- Why?

Participant D- It's just a geek brand, look how many features we can stick on it, or look how many vents we can stick on the side, loads of sharp edges on it, just seems really geeky

Interviewer- Is that what you associate with Sony then?

Participant D- Just everything on it seems over done

Interviewer- What sort of people do you think buy Sony then?

Participant D- Just teenagers really, who need all the latest techy stuff

Interviewer- What emotions do you align with Sony then?

Participant D- Frustration I think

Interviewer- What do you associate with Nokia then?

Participant D- I find them the most straight forward I think of all the phones, I would say they are reliable.

Interviewer- Have you ever had, or seen a mobile phone which displays your character a bit more?

Participant D- Yeah, I'll tell you which one I've always wanted, and that was the pebble phone, I think that was LG

Interviewer- It was Motorola

Participant D- Motorola Pebble

Interviewer- What was it about that which attracted you to it?

Participant D- Well, firstly the outside of it was gorgeous, and again when you opened it up it was fantastic

Interviewer- What do you associate with Motorola then?

Participant D- See, I wouldn't associate the pebble with Motorola, I didn't realise that was them, I thought that was somebody else

Interviewer- Do you see that as a standalone product, you don't see that as fitting in with a brand?

Participant D- I don't associate that with Motorola

Interviewer- OK, forgetting the pebble, what do you think of Motorola then?

Participant D- Similar to SonyEriccson, a kind of geeky, but a little bit rugged too, I think they do communication equipment for other things too

Interviewer- More of a utility product?

Participant D- Yeah, that's a really good way of putting it

Interviewer- Ok, so now the pebble has come along, do you think it has changed your perception of Motorola?

Participant D- No, because I haven't seen another phone by Motorola which has made me think its really nice.

Interviewer- Would you buy Motorola now based on that?

Participant D- No

Interviewer- Is the brand important to you, or is it the individual phone?

Participant D- Yeah, if its consistent, the individual item is really important to me though, like if SonyEriccson bought out a really sexy individual phone, and I liked it, then I would buy it, but I would sooner pick a Nokia or Samsung.

Interviewer- What do you associate with Samsung then?

Participant D- Well, their whole electronics range is just cool

Interviewer- Would you be willing to buy a Samsung phone then?

Participant D- Yeah, because I know the rest of their range is cool, I don't need to know all the individual phones in my head, because the Samsung stuff is gorgeous, like their tellys, I know that their phones will look quite cool as well.

Interviewer- Do you think they communicate their brand message a lot clearer than Motorola?

Participant D- yeah, absolutely, I think all their products are essentially pebbles. I know it's a safe bet because all their stuff is really nice.

Interviewer- What do you think of when you think of Samsung?

Participant D- Sleek, sexy, easy to use. I don't expect to be pissed off when I use a Samsung.

Interviewer- Do you find Samsung is quite in touch with you, what you aspire to?

Participant D- If you had to pick one brand out of all of them, Samsung would be me

Interviewer- I just think its quite sympathetic with its technology. Don't get me wrong, I like technology, but I don't want a swiss army knife of a phone. It just looks really polished and smooth. My SonyEriccson is horrible in my pocket, its nasty to use

Interviewer- Do you like any part of it?

Participant D- Yeah the camera

Interviewer- Why?

Participant D- Its just quite handy, its not a particularly good camera, and I'm not even sure how to get the pictures off it

Interviewer- So you wouldn't go back to Sony again?

Participant D- Nope, never

Interviewer- Have you ever had any other Sony products?

Participant D- yeah I had a Sony Hi-Fi

Interviewer- What was the first impression that phone had on you?

Participant D- To be honest, it was pretty good, it was a hell of a lot better than the other one I had, I'm guessing it was the camera which was why I really liked it.

Interviewer- Other than the camera, is there any other features you like?

Participant D- Not really. I can remember the packaging being nice, and when I first got it I thought the whole thing was nice.

Interviewer- So was the packaging adding to the whole experience of buying it?

Participant D- yeah it was nice, like the I-pod stuff, the packaging was really simple compared to the phone.

Interviewer- Do you think that anything which you liked in the packaging was in the phone, any consistency?

Participant D- No, the phones different, its not nice to use, I soon lost interest in it!

Interviewer- Do you admire the technology in the Sony stuff?

Participant D- yeah, the technology is quality, its all good quality stuff, like the TVs have good quality images, and the spec is good.

Interviewer- So why do you not like it then?

Participant D- Because its not fun, there's no link between the two. Its like the Sony Playstation has amazing graphics, but I'd much rather have a Wii

Interviewer- What products have you had which have really emotionally engaged you then?

Participant D- There is a router I've got at home which is not all techy, it looked nice to leave it out. That Philips light I bought was really nice

Interviewer- Do you associate Philips as emotionally engaging then?

Participant D- yeah I would

Interviewer - Do you think their technology is as good as Sony?

Participant D- I dunno, you're not aware of the technology, because it is so well delivered

Interviewer- How would you feel if you lost your phone then?

Participant D- Not that bothered, the only thing I would be annoyed about would be if I lost the sim-card

Interviewer- OK

Interviewer- If the brand was a person, who would it be?

Participant D- A geek, because I think of technology first with Sony, not pleasure to use

Interviewer- Can you remember your first encounter with Sony?

Participant D- Yeah my Dads old Hi-Fi, it was the same thing with it. Look, that's the remote (remote with lots and lots of buttons on it) The stereo has loads and loads of buttons on it, I'm not even sure what half the buttons do. It sounds really good, but my other one just had play stop pause.

Participant D- how does it make you feel using Sony?

Interviewer- Pissed off. It just makes me aware all the time it has so many functions.

Transcription of user interview 5

Interviewer- What would you say is the best thing about mobile phones?

Participant E- The mobility, the convenience. Its not just a mobile anymore really is it, its like a personal unit, you know, its got a calendar on it, I use it for the alarm, I use it as my mp3 player too. It does a lot of stuff really.

Interviewer- Would you say you are emotionally attached to the phone?

Participant E- I wouldn't say emotionally attached, its not like a watch or anything, but its more of a necessity.

Interviewer- How would you describe your phone to me as somebody who has never seen it?

Participant E-I would say it was simple and stylish, it's a Nokia, I've always had Nokia.

Interviewer- Why did you go for Nokia

Participant E- I'm not sure really, I've always had Nokias. I'm just so used to them, its weird, I don't think I could have another one really.

Interviewer- So, would you say you are more emotionally attached to the brand rather than the phone?

Participant E- Yeah, I suppose

Interviewer- how would you feel if Nokia were to go out of business and not do phones anymore?

Participant E- I suppose I would feel a bit sad you know

Interviewer- Can you explain why that is

Participant E- I dunno, I think its because its always been there, I've got used to them and I'm familiar with them.

Interviewer-Would you buy another Nokia phone?

Participant E- Yeah I think I would, although I think I might get an I-phone next

Interviewer- What is it about the I-phone which attracted you?

Participant E- I had a go on one, the styling is gorgeous, its intuitive, really nice usability, its great. Although, because I haven't got any money at the moment, I think I would have to just get a standard Nokia again.

Interviewer-Right I'm going to read you a list of brands, you have to tell me if you would buy them and what you associate with them. Ok Samsung?

Participant E- No, definitely not. My housemate had one, they're pretty tame, they've got crap features.

Interviewer- What do you associate with the Samsung brand?

Participant E- Not a lot really, I can't really say I know that much about them

Interviewer- Ok, LG

Participant E- Don't like them either, I remember playing with one that had crap touch buttons, which seemed really gimmicky, as you put the phone to your ear, and it rubs against it and hangs up. That's pointless. That actually put me off buying an LG TV when I was buying them, it stuck in my mind that much. It was pretty more than functional.

Interviewer- SonyEriccson?

Participant E- No. I think they are a bit cheap and nasty, like, they seem to have a lot of spray paint on them, when that chips off you've got grey plastic underneath. Whereas on my Nokia, its got actual black plastic, not plastic covered in paint. I prefer the use of honest materials.

Interviewer- How long have you had your current phone?

Participant E- I think I've had it about a year

Interviewer- What is it you like about it?

Participant E- Its simple, all honest use of materials, no grey paint, its got a nice metal frame on it which gives it this sense of quality, feels solid, and rigid. I like the simpleness of its use, and its really compact too which is nice for my pocket.

Interviewer- Is there anything you dislike about this phone?

Participant E- Yeah the camera on it is crap

Interviewer- What was it which made you buy this phone?

Participant E- I think it was the appearance, the brand, and it was at a perfect cost

Interviewer- What do you associate with Nokia?

Participant E- I think they're simple, they'vre got simple styling, I think that they're really easy to use as well, got a good user interface. I only found out the other day that they are Skandinavian, so I think of Ikea now as well, so I think of the whole design thing there and I can see now why I think its simple and elegant.

Interviewer- How would you feel if you lost this phone?

Participant E- I think I would be alright about it, cos you can replace it.

Interviewer- How would you feel if you scratched it

Participant E- That's funny because I think I would be more upset about that, because I try to look after it

Interviewer- Would you keep it or replace it?

Participant E- I would keep it, but I'd be upset. I think sometimes scratches are alright, because they tell a story.

Appendix E-Transcription of Interview with Designers

Transcription of designer interview 1

Interviewer-Can you consider please the following hypothetical situation, A well established brand wishes for you to aesthetically redesign n x product for them to fit in with their existing range. Can you briefly outline the methodology used to apply their brand traits on this product?

Respondent A- Right ok. Well the first thing we would do would be to make sure we are talking to the right people from that company, usually the marketing people. The work we do is usually part of a wider marketing campaign, so getting the people in who are deciding that will be our priority first, and make sure they are involved at every stage. It depends on which section of the company we are dealing with, you know, it could be audio rather than healthcare, so make sure we've got a good contact established there first.

Interviewer- What sort of help do they give you?

Respondent A- Well, I was just coming on to that. Usually, we are given some form of brand guidelines which would act as our starting point, then its up to us to pitch to them how far we can push the boundaries of that. Its all about making sure we are talking to the right people from day 1.

Interviewer- What are brand guidelines?

Respondent A- Its usually a document which either they have done to frame whatever we do. Its not particularly product base, but it has things in like what sort of colour range we could use and how big the logos should be, that kind of thing. As we are better at developing that sort of thing than they are, we usually pitch that to them as well to try and generate more income for us. There always needs to be evidence behind it though, because if we tear into the information which they think is perfectly fine with our own criticism, then we have to show them what would be better and why, and how it will help them generate more profit.

Interviewer- Are their brand guidelines usually well established?

Respondent A- Yeah, most of the time. But we can always develop it further. If it was a TV say to fit in with an existing range then we usually have to follow what we're given otherwise it will stand out. It all really depends on the marketing people and giving them enough options at each stage and making sure that they make the right decisions at each stage.

Interviewer- So, to summarise, in a situation like that, you would be given a set of guidelines for that range, and you would try to fit in with it as appropriately as possible?

Respondent A- erm, it depends what you mean by appropriate. It obviously needs to fit in. But if we are designing say a phone, to fit in with a range of cookers, for example, you cant just copy the same styling features across it a kind of pastiche way. You need to make sure whatever the brand is saying in the cooker is what they will say in the phone, sometimes it isn't always about adding the same curves or colours as they might not work on those scales.

Interviewer- So how would you make sure the brand is saying the same thiny?

Respondent A- We collate an awful lot of imagery as reference, of the brand, and identify which aspects say the same things. Then we take this across onto our phone! The other thing to consider is what year it will be coming out, its very different designing for 2012 than it is 2016!

Interviewer, ok, the second question-A well established brand wishes to progress/develop their existing brand language and apply it to a new product or range of products. Can you briefly outline the methodology used?

Respondent A- Ok, well again this is about how far you are allowed to push their brand guidelines. In this case we would usually push it a fair bit. In this situation, it is usually if the company is wanting to break into a new market, such as comfort, or luxury. We would need to understand the reason behind why they are doing it as well, so it would be about them telling us lots of stuff at the begging to make sure we're up to speed with all their marketing. The next thing would be to understand how long the range is going to be on the market for, how many products there are going to be, that sort of thing. Again, with timescales, if it has to be on the shelves for ages then it will have to look different than something which will be on the shelf for six months. The underlying concept is usually a driver on the whole thing...

Interviewer- Can you expand upon that?

Respondent A- Well, if it's a new technological innovation, then the design language needs to communicate something of that. Similarly, if its very ergonomic, then the language needs to communicate that too. Its again linking in what I said about what the marketing people are trying to do, and which market they are aiming for.

Interviewer- Ok, third situation. A new company with no particular brand language wishes for you to aesthetically (re)design x product for them. Can you outline the methodology used to establish their values in 3 dimensions?

Respondent A-The priority here would be for us to dictate to them what to do, because there is no point of being a consultancy and being told what to do. We'd make sure we again have all their correct people in the meetings, so the engineers, marketing people, because if we pitch to them a load of different languages, then they all need to know what is going on as they will be the ones taking the product further. Its also quicker like that as well. Their marketing people will usually have some keywords to describe the sort of thing their brand is about, which is a starting point for us. From there we are able to do mood boards, and collect lots of reference imagery which will translate into the design languages we come up with.

Interviewer- Can you expand upon how you use the imagery? Do you analyse it or break it down?

Respondent A- No not really, that's the kind of thing you see from students a lot, which is great, but when you do it for real you have more of a feel for it, it doesn't need to be as contrived as that.

Interviewer- Ok, to summarise, its about using marketing language and translating that into images?

Respondent A- yes. The keywords are really important for us and sometime we help them to develop them. For example, a lot of phones are now called 'pebble' or 'chocolate' rather than N3456. So we would look at what the semiotics are behind pebble, what pebbleness means culturally, which can sometimes mean different things in different contexts, and its about applying that meaning into form.

Interviewer- Can you elaborate on that at all?

Respondent A- Well, we would look at what the pebble means in society, you know, its just just about being a rock, is it about smoothness? Purity? Balance? Surface touch? That sort of thing. We would usually develop stories or narratives behind each of these meanings and these would be the drivers for the design. A pure looking phone would be meaning different things that say one which said balance, but they would both communicate pebbleness. Its about finding out which is the most appropriate to that market at that time.

OK, last question. 4-How important is it to involve target users (through interviews/focus groups) in the development of a brand language?

Respondent A-That's an interesting question! Erm, it tends to be more specific to one product that sort of thing. Its hard showing users a load of imagery or semiotics work as they tend not to get it. We would test a branding language with say one simple product, make some models, and apply different surface treatments, colours, finishes or forms and try and gauge what they are saying from that. It usually happens later on in the process.

Transcription of designer interview 2

Interviewer-Can you consider please the following hypothetical situation, A well established brand wishes for you to aesthetically redesign n x product for them to fit in with their existing range. Can you briefly outline the methodology used to apply their brand traits on this product?

Respondent B, right, well, usually we would have to get to know our client completely and the reasons why they are doing it. If they have a brand language already which we are subscribing to, then a lot of the forms, finishes and colours for example would be resolved already. This is a bit of an unusual situation, we have had it here before though, but what I can imagine has happened would be another company, or in-house team would have decided the previous range, or language there, in which case they would be the ones doing it again in most circumstances. However, if the company want to branch out into a say a microwave which would match its range of hobs, that could be more convincing. Its all about understanding why they want to do it and then we can go from there.

Interviewer- What tools and processes would you use to transfer the language from the cookers to the microwave? Do you analyse the forms first?

Respondent B- yeah, I mean, obviously we analyse the whole range, we familiarise ourselves completely with that range

Interviewer- Do you break the range into separate elements, such as colour, material, finish, form factor?

Respondent B- Yeah absolutely. It's only for us at the start though, we usually would get one of our design researchers to do that at the outset to give us a template to move forward with. That usually means breaking it into the surfaces we could use, the proportions, the finishes.

Interviewer- Is that done in a very rigid, analytical way or is it rather loose?

Respondent B- Well, I have seen approaches used in the past which are very strict. I worked at an automotive company for a while which was very strict in the balance of proportions, and the curvature of certain surfaces. Its because at that scale it is much much more obvious if a curve is on the piss compared to the rest of their cars. But here, we tend to keep it a bit loose. I think my Respondent Bs like having a bit of help pointing in the right direction, which is necessary of course as we are doing it for a particular brand, but we never really preach about having too much emphasis on getting everything really strict.

Interviewer- Do you feel it restricts them and stops their creativity?

Respondent B- yeah, absolutely. I mean, when getting the first, or even second round of concepts out, we don't want to have the blinkers on you know. To work at a place like xxxxxx, you need to have a good understanding of form and surface already, you would know by then what form means and how it evokes emotions, we need to keep these guys fresh and creative. The analysis we do at the beginning acts as reference, not so much as a rulebook. We get it right and keep our clients happy most of the time.

Interviewer, ok, the second question-A well established brand wishes to progress/develop their existing brand language and apply it to a new product or range of products. Can you briefly outline the methodology used?

Respondent B- Right, so a new language for a familiar brand?

Interviewer- Yes

Respondent B- Right, ok. Well again we need to understand why they are doing it, so that means talking to their marketing people and making sure why they want to do it. This is usually due to something changing first, such as a market, they might want to get into a new market, for example luxury. It's very unlikely that a company will want o uprgrade, if that's the right word, their brand language without any particular reason. Once we know the reason it gives us some direction and allows us to formulate the language from there.

Interviewer- What specific methods do you use to articulate this as form, or ingredients of form?

Respondent B- Well, usually this would mean having some kind of semiotic analysis done, whereby we look at say, luxury would mean. This means understanding the cultural discourses and codes behind 'luxury', really finding out what it means. Its fair enough sticking a load of images of luxury products on a board down, but to really do something which is appropriate you need to find what a particular strand of luxury is saying and match it to the values of that brand.

Interviewer- How you translate this into imagery?

Respondent B- Well, the imagery we collate would be used to illustrate the overall theme to the client. So, it may be 'modern luxury' to be crude, and those images we would show have a few example products which typify what we are getting at.

Interviewer- Do you analyse those images further, such as surfaces, colour breaks etc sp you have some reference for your Respondent Bs?

Respondent B- Yes, absolutely. Once they have chosen a route, a concept route, which I suppose could be considered a bit more of a marketing exercise in a way, we pool a lot of imagery , and have different banners of say finish, or silhouette. This is then used by the team to pick and choose at when they do their designs. To be honest, by the time we are ready to start sketching, the Respondent Bs would have spent hours collecting the images so its probably burnt onto their retinas! And, as I've said before, these are good Respondent Bs who have a fantastic sensitivity to form and they don't need a really explicit, dogmatic rule book to follow.

Interviewer- Ok, third situation. A new company with no particular brand language wishes for you to aesthetically (re)design x product for them. Can you outline the methodology used to establish their values in 3 dimensions?

,

Respondent B- Same as before really, we would see what the marketing team want to do, see why they are doing it, and from there we would collect imagery to represent what they are trying to say.

Interviewer- How important is it to involve target users (through interviews/focus groups) in the development of a brand language?

We never do it, I don't think they would understand it to be honest. We have trialled early products with users to see their response, but its not really something we can do because of confidentiality.

Transcription of designer interview 3

Respondent C- Well, we would need to establish why they were doing it first and foremost. This is a bit of a rare scenario, although it has happened. With the example you use of televisions here, paying a consultancy to do the design work for something which has already happened, if that makes sense, wouldn't be the wisest of things to do, because the point of us being a consultancy is we bring them an expertise they haven't had before. Saying that, if Sony in this example, had a successful range of televisions with this design language, and they wanted a range of DVD players or something to match it, then we might be able to offer assistance then. With regards to keeping the same language, again this is rare too because most products launch would require an innovation in there somewhere if it is high end. The lower end products which would use more modest technology, their in-house teams would look after them. I apologise if I am straying from the point but I thought I could clarify something for you there!

Interviewer- Ok, can we run with the hypothetical situation that Sony has a fairly new and successful TV range, and they have a new technology in DVD players which they would wish to match to the language of the TVS?

Respondent C- yes, I apologise for being a bit frank, ok that sounds good. Right, well we first need to establish why the bloody hell they are doing it! Although visually we would be matching the surface treatment, or the visual aspects of the range, the underlying concept, in this case new technology, would need to be communicated through the product as well. You can't just slap it on and hope for the best in this pastiche way. It will need to align, in spirit, what the televisions are saying visually with what the dvds have to say visually. It needs to go deeper.

Interviewer- what tools do you use to discover, and implement this 'spirit'.

Respondent C- Well, the marketing folk would tell us what they want to do in the way of matching it. But being a consultancy, we are usually approached to add something new. If we were given brand guidelines from their previous range and asked to go with that, great, we could get it out in two weeks no problem. But they usually want something new from us. So we would find what is it they want to say, which usually involves us being in a few meetings tearing our hair out really trying to coax out of them what they want to say, because its all well and could having it written on a piece of paper or report, but that's rarely what they want to do from their hearts. It usually means something else. What we're trying to communicate more is the other layers of meaning that an object can posses, that it can repeat its way of working with you. Its about creating a complete experience, not just an object. And this goes beyond just looks or branding. We begin I suppose by making sure we know what the consumer is like, so we have lots of ethnographic researchers, trends researchers looking at the market, and semioticians looking at the cultural baggage and codes attached to the objects.

Interviewer- I think you may be answering there my second question....

Respondent C- Oh right, well yea. Well we need to know what this cultural baggage is and find a way of usuing this for the brand. What a brand wants to communicate is very important. If it's a new area they are moving into, then we need to know why they want to do it. From there we do semiotics work to establish the meanings behind form. This is collated into boards, which are usually slides on powerpoints now, and these are given to our Respondent Cs as reference.

Interviewer- When you say meaning behind form, do you deconstruct it to see what the surfaces, or finish, or graphic treatments are of these reference images?

Respondent C Yes, but its done the other way around, if we need to say something is 'clean', there are many different meanings for clean, and what we do is identify what these meanings are and whether they can relate to that brand for the length of time they are willing to have it on the shelf for. It goes into meaning, which is what I think you are after, than what clean simply looks like. Its all rather deep, spiritual, and culturally relevant.

Question 3-

Interviewer- Are these the same techniques applied for....

Respondent C- yes

Interviewer- How important is it to involve target users in the development of brand languages?

Respondent C- We tend not to do it, as it usually infringes with client confidentiality.

Transcription of designer interview 4

Respondent D- Well, it depends who the brand is really. If it is a really familiar one who absolutely everyone will know, and if they have a huge market share, then that's going to be different than a smaller one

Interviewer- Ok, if it was Sony or Nokia say

Respondent D- Right, well we would have lots of meetings with their marketing managers to see what they were wanting to do first, where they want to go, and why they are doing it. If it was just say, design a new toaster to fit in with a range of kitchen equipment, we would just get a load of images of their existing range together and make sure were familiar with it, then just design a load of them and present them.

Interviewer- Do you do any form of form analysis or deconstruction?

Respondent D- Like semiotics and stuff? Not really. We don't really go that academic, in reality its more a case of just getting familiarising ourselves with the range and then giving them loads of options, its probably more efficient for use to do it like that.

Interviewer- Some consultancies have significant parts of their offer to clients as semiotic/brand analysis which dictates their design, do you not follow that?

Respondent D- We are only a small outfit, there is only four of us here full time, so we tend not to have time to do all that if we have lots of projects on. Personally, I have done it myself in a large consultancy, so it is something we have the capability to do, but not necessarily the capacity. Our main offer, if you like, to the client is just designing, and I think we do that very well. We tend to be able to do that a bit more instinctively, if we have their products in front of us already on a board, we can blast out a few options and they pick on which they think is the most appropriate.

Interviewer- So the existing imagery tends to be enough?

Respondent D- yeah

Question 2-

Respondent D- Ok, well we would again see what they want in terms of marketing spiel, such as what market its for, you know, if they were doing say a sports range we would go off and just design the whole range and present them a few options. This wouldn't be like properly designed products, we would just photoshop it, and they could all be subject to further development, but between the four of us, we would give them about 5 example ranges, and they might pick one or two for further development. From there we would get a few of the products in CAD and have them a bit more resolved and present them back to them.

Interviewer- How would imagery be used to influence this?

Designer- Well, for each example range we would have few images of example products around it. We have a folder on the shared drive with say, sporty1, sporty2 in there, and each would be a bit different, and these would give us some reference when designing the ranges.

Question 3-

Respondent D-Well, this is the same as before, we chat to their marketing guys and see what they want to do.

Interviewer- Do they have keywords which they might use to emphasise their brand

Respondent D- Yeah usually, we might then use these in an image search, collate a load of images and use them to inform the design, so we could have fast, or elegant or something on each board and design some products which emphasise that.

Interviewer- Do you visually break it down into say, surfaces, or graphic treatment?

Respondent D - No, you can get the feel of it just by looking at a load of pictures usually, its not really precise or academic in the real world. Well, not here anyway

Question 4

Respondent D- That's an interesting one. We have never done it, I don't really think the man on the street would get it, maybe he would, I'm not sure. I think we would just have issues with confidentiality which the client might not be happy about if we did.

DATE DUE	RETURNED

CPSIA information can be obtained at www.ICGtesting.com
Printed in the USA
LVOW120434081211

258395LV00002B/32/P

9 783844 310672